A BEGINNER'S GUIDE TO COLLECTING RARE COINS AND DISCOVERING VALUABLE ERRORS IN POCKET CHANGE

Build your collection from scratch and profit from it.

Carlos Clifton

Carlos Clifton

Copyright © 2023 Carlos Clifton

All rights reserved.

No part of this publication may be reproduced, distributed, or transmitted in any form or by any means, including photocopying, recording, or other electronic or mechanical methods, without the prior written permission of the publisher, except in the case of brief quotations embodied in critical reviews and certain other noncommercial uses permitted by copyright law.

Disclaimer: "A Beginner's Guide to Collecting Rare Coins and Discovering Valuable Errors in Pocket Change" is provided for informational and educational purposes only. While we strive to ensure the accuracy of the information, the world of coin collecting is ever-evolving, and coin values may fluctuate. The content is not intended as financial or investment advice and readers should conduct their own research and seek professional guidance for any financial decisions. Coin collecting and trading may involve risks, and individuals should exercise caution. The author and publisher are not responsible for any actions taken based on the information provided in the guide.

TABLE OF CONTENTS

TABLE OF CONTENTS 2

INTRODUCTION 5

CHAPTER ONE: GETTING STARTED IN COIN COLLECTING 7

    Understanding the Basics 8

    Historical Significance 11

    Types of Coins 18

    What Makes a Coin Rare and Valuable? 28

    Over Eight (8) Rules Of A Successful Coin Collecting 32

CHAPTER TWO: TOOLS AND RESOURCES FOR BEGINNERS 37

    Essential Tools and Supplies to Get You Started 38

CHAPTER THREE: GETTING STARTED: SETTING UP YOUR COLLECTION 47

    Choosing Your Focus: Periods, Mint Marks, and Denominations 50

CHAPTER FOUR: IDENTIFYING VALUABLE ERRORS IN POCKET CHANGE 53

    Recognizing Common Errors 54

    Types of Coin Errors 62

    Common Mint Error Coins 67

    20th Century Variety/Type Identifier Codes 77

CHAPTER FIVE: BUILDING YOUR COLLECTION FROM SCRATCH 81

    Budgeting for Coin Collecting: Tips for Beginners 82

CHAPTER SIX: CONNECTING WITH THE COIN COLLECTING COMMUNITY 85

    Joining Clubs and Associations 86

CHAPTER SEVEN: CARING FOR YOUR COLLECTION 91

    Proper Handling and Storage Techniques 91

CHAPTER EIGHT: GRADING YOUR COINS: A BEGINNER'S GUIDE 95

    Common Coin Grades 97

CHAPTER NINE: UNDERSTANDING MARKET VALUES 105

    How to Sell and Trade Error Coins 106

    How to Trade and Swap Coins 110

    Spotting Counterfeit Coins 112

CHAPTER TEN: THE MOST LOVED AND WIDELY COLLECTED COIN SERIES 115

    JEFFERSON NICKELS 115

    WASHINGTON QUARTERS 127

    LINCOLN PENNIES 141

    ROOSEVELT DIMES 153

    STATE QUARTERS 164

CHAPTER ELEVEN: ADVANCED TIPS FOR PROFITABLE COIN COLLECTING 175

    Investing in Rare Coins 175

CHAPTER TWELVE: COMMON PITFALLS AND HOW TO AVOID THEM 183

    Overcoming Beginner Mistakes 183

CONCLUSION **189**
   Celebrating Your Successes 189
   Continuing Your Journey in Coin Collecting............189
GLOSSARY **191**

INTRODUCTION

Have you ever wondered why people often overlook their pocket change? We absentmindedly toss coins into jars, drawers, or even spare change compartments, often dismissing their value. But what if I told you that some of those seemingly insignificant coins in your pocket are worth more than you might think? What if I shared a story of discovering hidden treasures in a family coin jar, sparking a newfound interest that led to a passion for coin collecting?

Imagine this: a simple jar of coins, a family heirloom filled with everyday pocket change. One day, while going through the coins absentmindedly, you stumble upon a peculiar one. It's not like the others; it has a flaw, an error that sets it apart. That moment, that discovery, marks the beginning of a journey into the fascinating world of coin collecting.

In this beginner's guide, I want to invite you to join me on this journey. Whether it's a casual interest or a potential hobby, coin collecting has the power to transport you to another world—one where every coin tells a unique story, and some of those stories can lead to accumulating wealth.

Why collect coins? For some, it's a passion or a hobby, and like all passions, it can open doors to a world of wealth accumulation. But where do you begin? How do you turn that jar of coins into something more? We aim to guide you through over ten rules of successful coin collecting.

In this guide, we'll show you how to perfectly identify a coin and recognize its value using the right tools suggested by experts. We understand that starting a collection can be daunting, so we've included clear photographs and images to make your coin-collecting journey not only educational but also visually engaging.

Imagine finding error coins in places you never thought to look. We'll reveal where to find coins for free and list various coin error types that could be hiding in your collection. Ever dreamt of stumbling upon a coin worth millions? We'll unveil over ten of the most valuable and rare coins that could potentially be sold for $12 million or more, along with tips on how to spot them.

But it's not just about finding valuable coins; it's also about making informed decisions when it comes to selling them. We'll guide you on how to spot fake coins and determine their market value, ensuring you navigate the world of coin collecting with confidence.

So, whether you're a curious beginner or someone looking to enhance their coin-collecting skills, this guide is for you. Get ready to uncover the secrets hidden within your pocket change, embark on a journey of discovery, and turn a jar of coins into a valuable collection that could be your ticket to a world of numismatic wonders.

CHAPTER ONE: GETTING STARTED IN COIN COLLECTING

Welcome to the fascinating world of coin collecting, where the jingle of loose change can lead to the discovery of hidden treasures. In this chapter, we'll explore the essentials of getting started in coin collecting, a passion that has evolved into a fast-growing endeavor offering both personal fulfillment and financial potential. Coin collecting, or numismatics, transcends a simple hobby—it's a journey into history, culture, and the thrill of discovery. Today, enthusiasts from diverse backgrounds find satisfaction and intellectual growth in the pursuit of acquiring new knowledge through coin collection.

Why should you collect coins today? It's more than assembling shiny metal discs; it's a multifaceted endeavor offering unique leisure time engagement, diversification for investment portfolios, and the potential for earning money through rare and valuable coins. The roots of coin collecting trace back centuries, with early collectors often being royalty and aristocrats. Today, it has become a widespread and inclusive hobby, accessible to individuals from all walks of life.

Understanding the basics involves grasping the fundamental components of a coin, from the head (featuring a prominent figure) to the tail (with various designs or symbols). Coins come in various types, from error coins with unique minting mistakes to brilliant uncirculated coins in pristine condition. Delving into the coin production process enhances our appreciation for these small but significant artifacts. What makes a coin rare and valuable lies in factors such as scarcity, historical significance, and condition.

As we navigate this chapter, we'll unveil over ten rules for successful coin collecting, drawing inspiration from the experiences of a successful coin collector—my grandfather. His journey from building a collection from scratch to accumulating wealth provides valuable insights into the principles that can guide your coin-collecting adventure. So, buckle up as we embark on this coin-collecting journey, where each coin is a doorway to history, a piece of art, and a potential source of both personal satisfaction and financial gain.

Understanding the Basics

What is coin collecting?

Hey there, welcome to the world of coin collecting! Now, you might be wondering, what exactly is this whole coin-collecting thing? Well, let's break it down in simple terms.

So, coin collecting is more than just grabbing a handful of coins and calling it a day. We've got a fancy word for it: numismatics. It's like a hobby on steroids—numismatics is the art and science of collecting coins. And trust me, it's not just about amassing shiny bits of metal. It's about diving into the stories these coins carry, the history they've witnessed, and the unique features that make them special.

Imagine it this way: you're not just collecting coins; you're collecting pieces of time, each with its tale. People dive into this because it's not just a hobby; it's a passion that spans generations. Whether you're in it for the thrill of discovering something new, the joy of handling these little treasures, or the knowledge you gain from digging into the past, numismatics has something for everyone.

And here's the cool part—it's a hobby that's growing fast. Like, fast. It's not just about filling up a coin jar; it's about recognizing the value of those coins. Some folks do it for the love of it, others see it as a way to diversify their investments, and some even turn it into a money-making venture. Yes, you heard it right—there's potential to earn some serious cash from collecting these little pieces of history.

So, as we start this journey into coin collecting, think of it as more than just a pastime. It's a way to connect with the past, understand the present, and maybe even secure your future. Get ready to uncover the stories behind each coin, because, in the world of numismatics, every coin is a piece of history waiting to be explored.

Who collects coins currently?

Alright, let's talk about who's into this whole coin-collecting gig these days. It's not just some niche thing; all sorts of folks are jumping on the bandwagon.

Who Collects Coins Today? Passionate Enthusiasts and Knowledge Seekers. First off, you've got the enthusiasts—those who turn coin collecting into a passion. They're not just after the coins; they're after the stories behind them. These are the folks who get a kick out of learning something new with every coin they add to their collection. It's like a treasure hunt, but instead of gold, they're after the thrill of discovering history in their hands.

And then some do it for the sheer joy of it. Imagine the excitement of finding a rare coin, the adrenaline rush of the hunt. These folks are in it for the physical pleasure, the excitement of exploring, and adding something unique to their stash. And get this, the whole process of searching and snagging new items for their collection can even trigger a bit of dopamine—yeah, the happy hormone. It's like a little reward for every cool coin they find.

A Fast-Growing Hobby with Earning Potential, Now, you might be thinking, "Why on earth would I start collecting coins?" Well, my friend, let me tell you—it's not just about having a bunch of cool coins. It's a fast-growing hobby, and there's more to it than meets the eye.

Firstly, it's not just about history; it's about the potential for some serious moolah. Yup, you read that right. People are making big bucks from their coin collections. Whether you're in it for the love of history or looking to diversify your investments, coins are like tiny treasure chests waiting to be cracked open.

Why You Should Collect Coins Today

So, why should you dive into this coin-collecting adventure? Well, for one, it's a hobby that spans the spectrum of satisfaction. You're not just collecting; you're absorbing history, getting a kick out of the hunt, and expanding your knowledge with each new addition.

And let's not forget the money part. Think of it as an investment. Your coin collection could be your secret stash for a rainy day. Plus, it's a way to diversify your portfolio and spread those financial eggs into different baskets. But here's the thing, it's not just about the money. It's about going beyond the usual reasons. It's about having a piece of history in your hands, about connecting with the stories of the past, and who knows, maybe even leaving a little something valuable for the next generation.

So, if you're up for a mix of passion, history, and maybe a bit of cash on the side, coin collecting is where it's at. Get ready to dive in and discover the world of coins—it's more than just a hobby; it's a journey through time in the palm of your hands.

Historical Significance

Alright, let's take a little stroll down the memory lane of coin collecting. The history of coins? It goes way, way back—like, ancient China back. The Chinese were rocking bronze coins around 800 BC to 1,000 BC. Then, Asians joined the coin party around 600 BC to 700 BC.

Fast forward to early America, and guess what? No coins in the pockets. Beaver skins, tobacco, and wampum were the OG currencies. But when foreign traders started rolling in, coins started making the rounds in the U.S. By the 18th century, Americans were minting their copper coins. The U.S. Mint, the cool place where coins are born, kicked off operations in Philly in 1793.

Now, when did people start collecting these little pieces of metal? Well, probably since the first coins ever showed up. But the earliest known coin collector we can point to is the Roman Emperor Augustus, way back from 63 BC to 14 AD. In the Middle Ages and early American history, only rich kids could afford to collect coins. Everyone else was busy spending coins on life essentials like food and clothing. Fast forward to today, and coin collecting is a bustling hobby for all. You don't need a fat wallet to start a collection—kids are even in on the action.

Now, my coin-collecting journey started back in the early '90s. Picture this: no 50 State Quarters program, coin prices were bouncing back from a dip, and designs on circulating U.S. coins hadn't changed for ages. It was a bit quiet in the coin-collecting world. But then, here comes the hero: the U.S. quarter! Back in the middle of the 20th century, coin collecting hit its golden era. The '50s and '60s were the sweet spot for collectors. You could find old, even rare coins just by checking your pocket change. Mercury dimes, Indian Head pennies, Buffalo nickels—they were all up for grabs.

But wait, the party came to a halt. In the '60s, silver coins phased out, and collectors swooped in to grab what was left. The number of collectors seemed to stall, if not drop. Interest would spark here and there, but the '80s coin investment excitement soured, and the '90s were kind of meh for coin collecting.

Then, cue the drumroll, the U.S. Mint unleashed the 50 States Quarters Program in 1999. It was like a coin-collecting revival! Tens of millions hopped on the coin-collecting train, and it wasn't just about quarters. The government even jumped on the bandwagon, approving more programs like D.C. and U.S. Territories Quarters and U.S. National Parks Quarters.

So, why collect coins today? It's not just about history or making a quick buck. It's about the joy of discovery, connecting with the past, and maybe even leaving something valuable for the future. The U.S. quarter, with its ever-changing designs, keeps the coin-collecting flame alive, potentially sparking joy in collectors until the 2030s.

Oh, and ever wondered where a coin has been? Imagine the stories it could tell—from first dates to milkshake runs. It's a whole adventure in your pocket. Happy collecting!

Anatomy of a Coin

Now, let's talk about the anatomy of a coin because before you dive into the world of coin collecting, it's handy to know what's what. It's like getting to know the characters in a story.

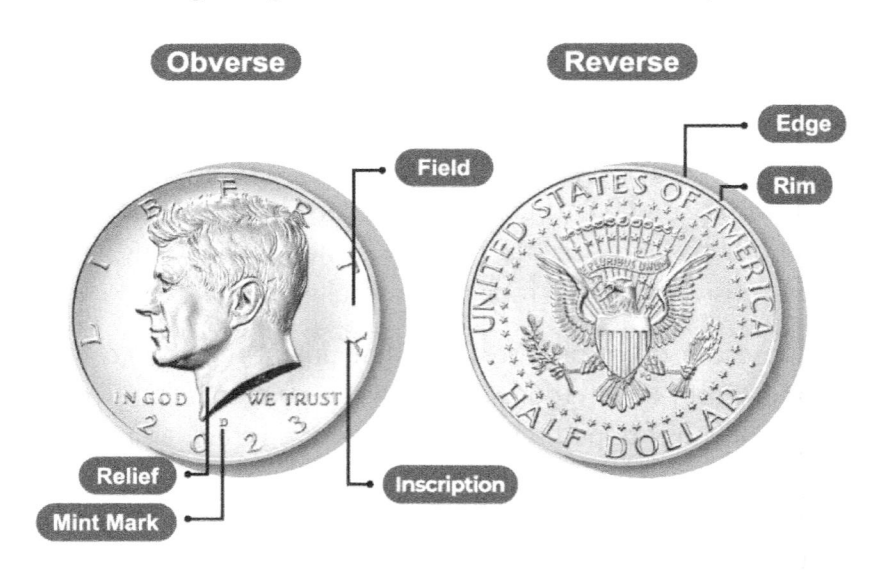

Basic Components or Parts of a Coin:

1. **Obverse:** This is the main actor, the front side, often called the "heads." It's where you find the date and the portrait design—the face of the coin.

2. **Reverse:** Flip it over, and you've got the "tails." This is the other side of the coin, offering a different perspective.

3. **Edge:** Think of the edge as the frame of the coin. It's the outer border, and it can come plain, reeded (with grooves), have lettering, or even some fancy decorations.

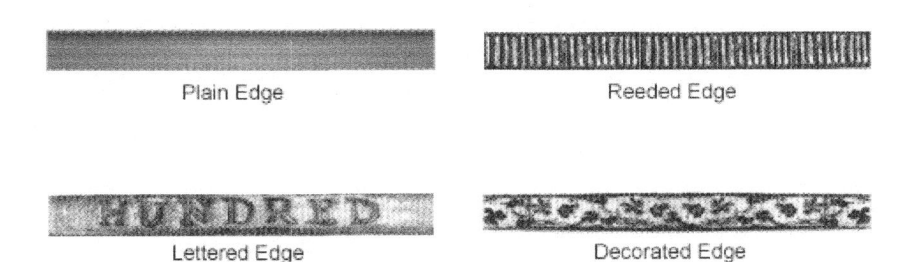

Plain Edge

Reeded Edge

Lettered Edge

Decorated Edge

4. **Rim:** Picture a protective barrier. The rim is the raised part of the edge on both sides of the coin, shielding the design from the wear and tear of everyday use.

5. **Inscription:** Now, this is the main dialogue. The principal words or lettering on a coin, also known as the legend. It tells a bit of the coin's story.

6. **Mint Mark:** Ever wondered where a coin was born? The mint mark is a small letter or symbol indicating its birthplace. In the U.S., you might spot P (Philadelphia), D (Denver), S (San Francisco), or W (West Point).

7. **Relief:** Imagine this as the 3D effect. The relief is the part of a coin's design that's raised above the surface, giving it depth and character.

8. **Field:** This is like the stage background. The flat part of a coin's surface is not used for design or inscription but for setting the scene.

More on the Parts of a Coin:

Now, let's meet some supporting characters that add layers to our coin story:

- **Portrait or Bust:** Here's the main character in detail. It's the heart of a coin's design, showcasing presidents, royalty, or symbolic figures.
- **Field:** The area surrounding the main action, on proof coins, it can be polished to a mirror-like finish, making the central design pop.
- **Motto:** The supporting lines, like a catchy tagline. It's secondary lettering conveying a saying or short phrase, injecting a bit of personality.
- **Date:** Every coin has its birthday. The date signifies when it was struck. Some coins, especially historical or commemorative ones, might have dual dates.
- **Designer's Initials:** The artist's signature, tucked away in small letters. Not all coins let the designer sign their work, but when they do, it adds a personal touch.
- **Denomination:** Think of this as the coin's role. It's the face value, like One Dollar or Ten Pounds, determining its place in the currency world.

Why Does It Matter?

Learning the parts of a coin isn't just about impressing your friends—it adds to the joy of inspecting your collection. The U.S. Silver Eagle we're talking about here is just one example. Keep in mind, that different countries and coins may mix up these parts a bit, and not every coin has all the parts we've listed.

So, when you're admiring your coins, remember you're not just holding pieces of metal. Each one is a mini work of art with its cast of characters, and knowing who's who makes the collection even more fascinating.

Coin Finishes: Dressing Coins in Style

Now, let's talk about the different outfits coins wear—yes, I'm talking about their finishes. Think of it like dressing up your coins for different occasions.

Uncirculated | Proof | Reverse Proof

Examples of Uncirculated proof and reverse proof finishes

Coin Finishes: Dressing Coins in Style

1. **Circulating Coins: Everyday Attire**
   - These are the coins that mingle with us in our daily hustle of buying and selling.
   - They're made by the Mint without any extra fancy steps. Just regular, everyday coins doing their job.

2. **Uncirculated Coins: Ready for the Spotlight**

- Mint makes these for collectors and savers. They're like the A-listers of coins.
- Produced similar to circulating coins, but with a little extra flair for that brilliant finish. It's like giving them a VIP pass to stand out.

3. **Proof Coins: The Shiny Stars**
   - Picture this—mirror-like background with frosted design elements. Now, that's a coin making a statement.
   - The Mint goes all out, manually feeding burnished coin blanks into presses with polished dies. Each coin gets struck at least twice for that extra wow factor.

4. **Reverse Proof Coins: The Trendsetters**
   - These coins flip the script—a frosted background with a mirror-like design. It's like having a coin with a bold fashion statement.
   - They stand out in the crowd, turning the usual design order on its head.

Enhanced Finishes: Adding Extra Sparkle

- Sometimes, the Mint likes to sprinkle a bit of magic on certain coins—call them the showstoppers.
- They apply frosting or polishing to specific areas, bringing out even more detail. It's like putting on a highlighter to make those features pop.

So, there you have it—the different styles of coins rock. From everyday casual to red carpet-ready, each coin finish tells a unique story. It's not just about the metal; it's about the presentation. And just like us, coins like to dress up for special occasions, making each one a little work of art in your collection.

Types of Coins

Coins aren't just pocket change; they're tiny storytellers, each with its unique tale. Let's unravel the diverse world of coins, simplifying the jargon for everyone to grasp.

1. Currency Coins: The Everyday Heroes

These are the coins you use daily—pennies, nickels, dimes, and quarters. Different metals give them distinct sizes, weights, and looks. They're like the reliable sidekicks of your shopping adventures.

2. Commemorative Coins: The Superheroes

Imagine coins celebrating historical figures or marking special events. Commemorative coins are like the superheroes of the coin world, beautifully designed and turning moments into valuable collectibles.

3. Bullion Coins: Tiny Treasures of Wealth

Made of precious metals like gold and silver, bullion coins are investments. Their value is based on metal content, not face value. It's like having tiny treasures that can grow your wealth over time.

4. Tokens: The Special-Use Coins

Tokens are like coins with a specific mission. Arcade tokens for games, subway tokens for transportation—they serve unique purposes and are often made of materials like plastic or brass.

5. Ancient Coins: Time-Traveling Adventures

Hold a piece of history with ancient coins from civilizations like Greece and Rome. Each coin whispers tales of the past, offering a time-traveling adventure for collectors.

6. Error Coins: Rare Misprints

Imagine coins with quirks—misaligned designs, double-stamped images. Error coins are rare misprints with intriguing stories, sought after by collectors for their uniqueness.

7. Proof Coins: The Showstoppers

Proof coins are the red carpet stars. Specially minted to showcase top-notch craftsmanship, they have mirror-like surfaces and sharp details, often stored in protective cases.

8. Foreign Coins: Mini Globetrotters

Foreign coins are like mini travelers from around the world. Collecting them is a journey through different cultures and histories, discovering colorful representations of countries.

9. Novelty Coins: The Tricksters

Novelty coins are playful tricksters. Unusual shapes, holes in the middle, hidden surprises—they're created for fun and make quirky collectibles.

10. Limited Edition Coins: Rare Gems

Like rare Pokémon cards, limited edition coins are produced in small quantities, making them highly sought after. Part of a series or theme, they're great investments due to their scarcity.

Conclusion: A Rich Tapestry of Coins

Coins cater to all interests—collectors, investors, or those who love history. From everyday heroes like currency coins to the allure of ancient coins and the playfulness of novelty coins, there's a coin for everyone. The next time you hold a coin, take a moment to appreciate its unique story and the role it plays in our world. You might just uncover a newfound passion for collecting these tiny treasures!

The U.S Mint Marks

Coins have stories to tell, and one crucial detail adding depth to their tales is the tiny mark that often goes unnoticed—the mint mark. Let's unveil the mystery behind those small letters stamped on U.S. coins.

Understanding Mint Marks: The Unseen Significance

In the coin world, "mint" is a term that echoes in various contexts. There's the U.S. Mint, the production powerhouse for the nation's coinage. Mint coins, pristine from the U.S. Mint facility, signify top-notch condition. Mint sets compile uncirculated coins from a specific year. Lastly, there are mint marks, our focus here, those inconspicuous letters that carry a coin's birthplace identity.

List of U.S. Mint Marks:

- **C – Charlotte Mint:** North Carolina (gold coins only from 1838-1861)

- **CC – Carson City Mint:** Nevada (gold and silver coins only from 1870-1893)

- **D – Dahlonega Mint:** Georgia (gold coins only from 1838-1861)

- **D – Denver Mint:** Colorado (from 1906-present)

- **O – New Orleans Mint:** Louisiana (gold and silver coins only from 1838-1861 and from 1879-1909)
- **P – Philadelphia Mint:** Pennsylvania (from 1793-present)
- **S – San Francisco Mint:** California (from 1854-present, primarily struck proof coins from 1968)
- **W – West Point Mint:** New York (from 1984-present)

It's interesting to note that while mint marks like "D" represent Denver, certain coins, especially gold coins, may require distinguishing between Dahlonega "D" and Denver "D" based on the date.

Where to Find Mint Marks on U.S. Coins: Mint marks have found their place in various locations on coins over the years. Here are some common locations for popular coins:

- **Buffalo Nickels:** On the reverse, below the words FIVE CENTS.
- **Lincoln Cents:** On the obverse, beneath the date.
- **Silver Trade Dollars, Silver Peace Dollars, Silver Morgan Dollars, Silver Bust Dollars:** Underneath the eagle on the reverse
- **Kennedy Half Dollars (Pre-1965):** On the reverse, left of the olive branch near the eagle's claw; (1968-present): On the obverse, centered above the date
- **Franklin Half Dollars**: On the reverse, centered above the beam of the Liberty bell

- **Washington Quarters (1968-present):** On the obverse, bottom right next to the hair ribbon; (1946-1964): On the reverse, below the eagle
- **Roosevelt Dimes (1968-present):** On the obverse, above the date; (1946-1964): On the reverse, bottom left of the torch
- **Jefferson Nickels (1968-present):** On the obverse, near the date; (1938-1964): On the reverse, right of the Monticello building
- **Buffalo Nickels:** On the reverse, below "FIVE CENTS"
- **Lincoln Cents:** On the obverse, beneath the date

While most U.S. coins have mint marks, exceptions include some coins struck at the Philadelphia Mint and certain error coins.

History and Quirks of Mint Marks: The usage of mint marks has not been consistent throughout history. For instance, the Philadelphia Mint only introduced the "P" mintmark in 1942, and it became regular after 1978. Notably, coins made at the Philadelphia Mint historically lacked mint marks.

U.S coins without mintmarks

In conclusion, those seemingly inconspicuous mint marks tell a story of a coin's origin, and understanding them adds a layer of intrigue to the fascinating world of coin collecting. Whether you're inspecting a silver dollar or a Lincoln cent, knowing where to find the mint mark unveils a piece of the coin's journey through time.

Coin Production and the Steps Involved

Welcome to the mesmerizing world of coin production, where raw materials transform into the familiar currency jingling in our pockets. This intricate process, orchestrated by the U.S. Mint, involves a symphony of machines and precise techniques across four facilities in Philadelphia, Denver, San Francisco, and West Point. From the artistic inception of a coin's design to the rhythmic dance of presses striking millions of coins daily, join us on a journey through the fascinating steps that birth the coins we use, collect, and cherish. It's more than just metal; it's the alchemy of craftsmanship and technology shaping the currency that connects us all.

Ever wondered how those coins jingling in your pocket come to life? Let's take a fascinating journey into the heart of coin production at the U.S. Mint and unravel the intricate steps involved.

Step 1. Design Approval and Sculpting

The coin creation process kicks off with the Secretary of the Treasury green-lighting a design. Talented Mint artists then transform a two-dimensional sketch into a three-dimensional sculpture. Once finalized and digitized, this sculpture becomes the blueprint for the coin dies responsible for imprinting the design onto the coins.

Step 2. Blanking: From Metal Coils to Blanks

The birth of a coin begins with the creation of blanks—flat metal discs that will metamorphose into coins. For nickels, dimes, quarters, half dollars, and dollars, the Mint crafts these blanks by feeding metal coils through a straightening machine and then a blanking press. This press, operating at a remarkable speed of 14,000 blanks per minute, shapes the metal into coin-sized blanks. Pennies, numismatic, and bullion coins, however, opt for pre-purchased blanks.

Step 3. Annealing: Preparing for Striking

To ready the blanks for striking, they undergo annealing, a process that imparts flexibility to the metal. The blanks endure intense heat, up to 1,600 degrees Fahrenheit, in an oxygen-free environment. A quick dip in a quench tank, filled with a special "slippery" water concoction, cools them rapidly, preventing tarnishing.

Step 4. Washing and Drying: Restoring Shine

Post-annealing, the blanks get a bath to restore their original color, using a mixture of cleaning and anti-tarnish agents. A steam dryer then ensures the blanks are impeccably dried before moving on to the next stage.

Step 5. Upsetting: Crafting the Raised Rim

Upsetting involves creating a raised rim, a protective edge for the coin. The blanks enter an upsetting mill, where a groove slightly narrower than their diameter shapes the metal around the edge, forming the rim or what is now known as a planchet.

Step 6. Striking: Bringing Designs to Life

The planchets proceed to coin presses for the grand finale—the striking of the design. With varying degrees of pressure, depending on the denomination, the press forces the obverse and reverse dies against the planchet. The metal flows into the design, and a collar prevents excessive expansion, forming the coin's edge design.

Circulating coin presses work at speeds of up to 750 coins per minute, resulting in millions of coins each day. Proof coins, destined for collectors, undergo at least two strikes for enhanced detail.

Step 7. Inspection and Waffling: Quality Assurance

Inspector scrutiny follows striking, with samples examined for errors. If the coins pass inspection, they move to packaging. However, if circulating coins fall short of standards, they face a unique fate—a trip to the waffler. This machine imparts wavy lines to the coins before they head for recycling.

Step 8. Bagging and Packaging: Ready for Circulation

Circulating coins, after being counted and weighed, find themselves funneled into bulk storage bags, awaiting distribution to Federal Reserve Banks. Meanwhile, numismatic coins receive meticulous packaging treatment, courtesy of robots and automated machines, before landing on shelves for collectors. Bullion coins, housed in monster boxes, are packaged for shipment to authorized dealers.

And there you have it—the intricate dance of creativity, precision, and technology that transforms raw metal into the coins we use every day. The next time you hold a coin, remember the remarkable journey it took to reach your hands. Happy coin collecting!

What Makes a Coin Rare and Valuable?

Have you ever wondered why some coins are considered valuable while others might just be pocket change? It's not just about how old a coin is – there's a whole fascinating world behind what makes a coin truly precious. Welcome to the fascinating realm of coin valuation, where the worth of these small treasures is far from a straightforward equation. In this journey, guided by the insights of Joshua McMorrow-Hernandez, we'll unravel the mysteries behind what makes coins truly valuable.

Carlos Clifton

Why Are Coins Valuable In the First Place?

Coins, at their core, are more than just pieces of metal; they are tangible currency, a reflection of financial systems and historical epochs. In the annals of history, coins derived their value from metallic composition, a concept now overshadowed by fiat money, where their worth is declared by governments. Yet, the allure of modern bullion and vintage gold or silver coins lies in their intrinsic precious metal content, often far exceeding their face value. Furthermore, the realm of collectibles breathes new life into coins, adding a layer of value beyond mere currency. Let's delve into the key factors that elevate a coin's value.

1. The Coin's Bullion Value: Most United States coins are crafted from metals like copper, nickel, gold, silver, and platinum, each carrying intrinsic value. The bullion value, or the metal's inherent worth, is a major player in a coin's overall value. Notably, coins like old copper pennies, pre-1965 silver coins, silver dollars, and certain gold coins are prized not just for their face value but for the precious metals they contain.

2. The Coin's Rarity: A coin's rarity is a crucial factor, determined by its mintage – the number of coins initially produced. While low mintage generally implies rarity, it's not the whole story. Consider the estimated number of survivors or population, which factors in coins lost to melting or other causes. For instance, the 1933 Saint-Gaudens double eagles, despite a seemingly high mintage, became exceedingly rare due to legal requirements that led to most being melted.

3. Demand for the Coin: Rarity alone doesn't dictate a coin's value; demand plays a vital role. Take the 1909-S VDB Lincoln penny, with a mintage of 484,000. Despite its relative abundance, high demand from collectors makes it more valuable than coins with lower mintages. The number of collectors vying for a particular coin can significantly influence its market value.

1909-S "VDB" Lincoln Wheat cent

4. Errors or Varieties on the Coin: Not all oddities diminish a coin's value; true errors and varieties can make a coin more valuable. The 1955 doubled die penny, a famous error, is worth over $1,000. Off-center strikes, broad strokes, and off-metal errors are examples of anomalies that collectors find intriguing and valuable.

5. The Condition (or Grade) of the Coin: A coin's condition is a key determinant of its value. Well-preserved coins, known as conditional rarities, can be more valuable despite common mintage. Grading services like NGC and PCGS assess a coin's condition, considering wear, damage, and overall appeal. Even modern coins, if preserved in mint condition, can hold significant value.

6. Design: The cultural, historical, and patriotic themes encapsulated in a coin's design can enhance its appeal and value, especially if the design holds significance or is part of a limited edition.

The reverse design of the Eisenhower Dollar celebrated the recent moon landing.

7. **Age**: Older coins tend to become scarcer as time erodes their numbers, and age-associated factors like wear and rarity come into play.

Other Factors to Consider

- **Errors**: Genuine mint-made errors can render a coin exceptionally rare and valuable, distinguishing it from its regular counterparts.
- **Provenance**: A coin's lineage, whether it had a famous owner or was part of a significant hoard, can add a historical premium to its value.

How Do I Know If My Coin Is Valuable?

Identifying the country of origin, deciphering the date, and understanding the denomination are the initial steps in coin identification. Further exploration into unique features, such as errors or limited editions, can be conducted with the guidance of a numismatic expert. Local coin dealers or numismatists can provide insights and reasonable estimates regarding the value of your coin, transforming a simple piece of metal into a potentially valuable artifact.

While age, design, and bullion content also contribute to a coin's worth, these five factors are at the heart of what makes a coin truly stand out in the world of numismatics. So, the next time you come across an old coin, take a moment to consider its journey and the unique elements that might just make it more valuable than you think.

Over Eight (8) Rules Of A Successful Coin Collecting

Let me share a story about my grandfather, a man who turned his passion for coin collecting into a thriving source of wealth. Starting with nothing but a keen interest, he embraced this hobby wholeheartedly and built his collection from scratch. His success wasn't just about amassing coins; it was a journey guided by a set of principles that transformed his collection into a valuable asset. These are the ten rules he ardently followed, shared by numismatist Doug Winter.

The 10 Rules of Successful Coin Collecting

Rule I. Education

The foundation of successful coin collecting lies in education. Grandpa immersed himself in numismatics, studying not only coins but also the market dynamics. Books, catalogs, and memberships in associations like the American Numismatic Association were his tools. He connected with fellow collectors, asked questions, and continuously expanded his knowledge.

Rule II. Specialization

He believed in setting clear goals and boundaries. Starting with a specific focus, like Charlotte gold coinage, made the vast world of coins more manageable. Specialization, he emphasized, levels the playing field with dealers and facilitates better-informed purchases.

Rule III. Patience

In a world of instant gratification, Grandpa understood the power of patience. Building a remarkable coin collection takes years. Impulsive decisions, he warned, often lead to regrettable choices. True value, he insisted, comes to those who wait.

Rule IV. Connections

He valued firsthand information over third-hand sources. Building connections with well-connected, reliable dealers was crucial. Real insights into pricing, market conditions, and trends came from those actively participating in shows and auctions.

Rule V. Thinking Like a Collector

Grandpa believed in the heart of a collector. He stressed the importance of buying coins for the right reasons—love and genuine interest. Acting like a true collector, he asserted, ensures not only enjoyment but also the potential for reasonable profits.

Rule VI. Connoisseurship

The ability to recognize true quality, or connoisseurship, was another aspect he highlighted. Grandpa could appreciate the aesthetic appeal of coins and distinguish exceptional pieces. For those not born connoisseurs, he suggested seeking assistance from knowledgeable dealers.

Rule VII. Learning to Grade

Grading was a skill he considered indispensable. He advised aspiring collectors to attend shows, take grading classes, specialize, and learn from dealers. Third-party grading was a safety net, but nothing replaced personal knowledge.

Rule VIII. Thinking Long Term

Coins, he emphasized, were a long-term investment. Holding onto them for at least a decade was a prudent approach. He drew parallels with legendary collections like Eliasberg and Pittman, built over fifty years.

Rule IX. Quality Not Quantity

Quality surpassed quantity in his rulebook. He suggested investing in a few outstanding coins rather than a multitude of average ones. As the market evolved, he predicted that high-quality coins would become scarcer and more valuable.

Rule X. Buying the Best You Can

For newcomers, he advocated starting small. Studying the market for three to six months before delving into significant purchases was his wise counsel. Understanding one's limitations and gradually navigating the market proved essential.

Conclusion

Grandpa's approach wasn't easy, requiring discipline and a substantial time commitment. While not everyone may follow every step, incorporating these principles gradually can lead to a richer understanding of numismatics. If some steps resonate with you now and others don't, remember them as you embark on your journey in the world of coin collecting.

CHAPTER TWO: TOOLS AND RESOURCES FOR BEGINNERS

Embarking on a journey into the world of coin collecting doesn't mean diving into a sea of complicated gadgets or fancy contraptions. In fact, the tools you need to kickstart your coin collecting adventure have remained refreshingly simple, despite centuries of coin collecting history. This chapter is your guide to the indispensable tools and resources that will make your foray into the realm of coins both enjoyable and rewarding.

Assembling a toolkit doesn't have to break the bank. It's like building your coin collection – start with the basics and gradually add more sophisticated tools as your journey unfolds. The wisdom shared here comes not just from any source but from the insights of seasoned experts in error coin collecting. These tools are not just recommendations; they are the trusted companions of those who have navigated the intricate world of coin varieties and errors.

There's a saying in the coin-collecting community: "Start small, but dream big." The tools discussed in this chapter are the embodiment of that philosophy. They cater to both the novice collector and the seasoned enthusiast, aiding in the discovery of those small but significant nuances that make a coin truly special.

Errors and varieties, those hidden treasures waiting to be unearthed, often hide in plain sight. They're small, and to uncover their secrets, you need the right tools. Magnification becomes your ally, revealing the intricate details that set one coin apart from the rest. So, let's delve into the toolkit – over ten essential tools, their prices, and where to find them – carefully curated to make your searching easier and your coin-collecting journey more fulfilling.

Get ready to equip yourself with the knowledge and tools that will turn your passion for coins into a captivating adventure. Whether you're on a budget or ready to invest in your collection, these tools will be your companions in the fascinating realm of coin varieties and errors. Let's dive in, explore, and uncover the mysteries that each coin holds, armed with the right tools for the job.

Essential Tools and Supplies to Get You Started

So, you've caught the coin collecting bug, and now you're wondering, "What do I need to get started?" The truth is, there's no one-size-fits-all answer because every collector has their unique purpose. Whether you're a curious child, a passionate enthusiast, or maybe even considering turning your hobby into a source of income like a dealer, the tools you need will evolve with your journey. Let's break down the essentials, starting from the basics.

1. Lighting: Illuminating the Details

Imagine trying to decipher the secrets of a coin in the dim glow of a cloudy day. Not ideal, right? That's where lighting comes into play. To truly see and understand your coins, you need adequate illumination. Here's why:

- **Dirt and Grime:** Coins can gather dirt, hiding crucial details. Lighting exposes these imperfections.

- **Wear and Tear:** Worn-out coins might have faint dates. Proper lighting reveals these subtle features.

- **Trauma Damage:** Scratches, dents, or gouges – these affect a coin's identity. Good lighting brings them to light.

- **Tiny Features:** Some features are minuscule. Only with ample lighting can you spot them.

- **Shadows:** Poor lighting creates shadows, obscuring details. The solution? Good lighting.

Specifications for the Light Source:

Forget fluorescent lights; they're too soft. "Natural" light is a no-go too. Opt for a 75-watt incandescent bulb. It's the gold standard, revealing blemishes, mint characteristics, and damages. Now, let's brighten up your coin-collecting journey.

2. Magnifying Glass: Bringing the Minuscule to the Forefront

Just as important as good lighting is a trusty magnifying glass. This little wonder helps in authentication, grading, and spotting hidden features. Here's the breakdown:

Three Types of Magnifiers:

- **Traditional Handheld Magnifier:** Start here. A 1.5 to 4-inch diameter glass with a built-in secondary lens (5x to 7x) unveils details.

- **Sewer's Magnifier:** Get hands-free with foundation clamps. Ideal for thorough inspections using both hands.

- **Jeweler's Loupe:** As your collection expands, invest in a loupe with 10x to 15x magnification for precise scrutiny.

Remember, you might not need all three types at the beginning. Start with the basics and let your collection guide your tool upgrades. Illuminate, magnify, and discover the captivating world of coins, one detail at a time. Happy collecting!

3. Gloves

Coins, though made of metal, are surprisingly sensitive to dirt, oils, and acids from your skin. To safeguard your coins, gloves are a must-have. Ensure you're wearing them when handling coins that are in mint condition, uncirculated, feature commemorative images or insignias, or have an exceptionally clean or polished surface.

Recommended Types of Gloves:

- **Soft Cotton Gloves (white):** Simple, washable, and disposable finger protection.
- **Powder-free Latex Gloves:** Non-reactive coverings for your fingers.

- **Nitrile Gloves:** Highly flexible, sensitive, and resistant to chemicals, usually in blue.

- **Finger Cots:** Cover one or more fingers, made from latex, nitrile rubber, or vinyl – use only if no other options are available.

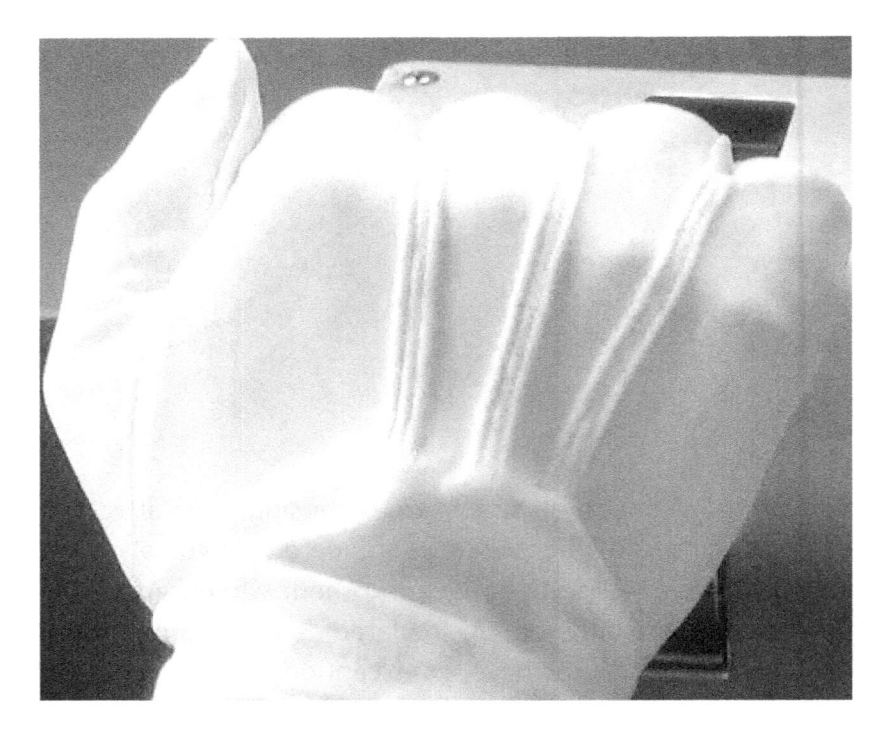

Why This Matters: While some may associate hand protection with only high-value coins, the oils and acids on your skin can leave deposits on any coin's surface, regardless of its value. These deposits can lead to discoloration and damage over time. Hand protection also prevents dirt accumulation, maintaining the coin's integrity. This can be purchased for $6 on harbor freight or you can get it on Amazon.

4. Viewing Pad

Coins, resilient as they are, can still be susceptible to damage, especially when handling uncirculated or mint edition coins with highly polished face plates. To prevent scratches or dulling, use a soft surface like a cotton pad or washcloth when examining coins. Placing the coin flat on this cushioned surface ensures protection and prevents it from rolling or sliding on hard surfaces, crucial when showcasing coins to others without any casing.

As you embark on your coin collecting journey, these tools become your allies, preserving the beauty and value of your coins. Remember, the small steps you take in protection today can lead to the longevity and appreciation of your coin collection tomorrow.

5. Digital Scale

Planning to buy or sell coins? A digital scale is your ally in ensuring legitimacy. It's not just about weighing coins; it helps discern error coins or clad coins, especially during transitional periods like the shift from silver to clad quarters. Knowing the weight difference between solid metal and clad coins becomes crucial for transactions involving coins from transitional years. This can be purchased for $10 on Amazon.

Carlos Clifton

6. Digital Caliper

Picture this as your coin's personal tailor. The digital caliper is a sizing wizard that measures the diameter of your coins. Why is this important? Well, it helps you identify if a coin was minted from a collar, had a broad strike, or came from an improper planchette. Knowing these details can determine the value of your coins. Some may be worth their face value, while others could fetch a pretty penny. Keep this tool handy to unveil the secrets hidden in the size of your precious coins.

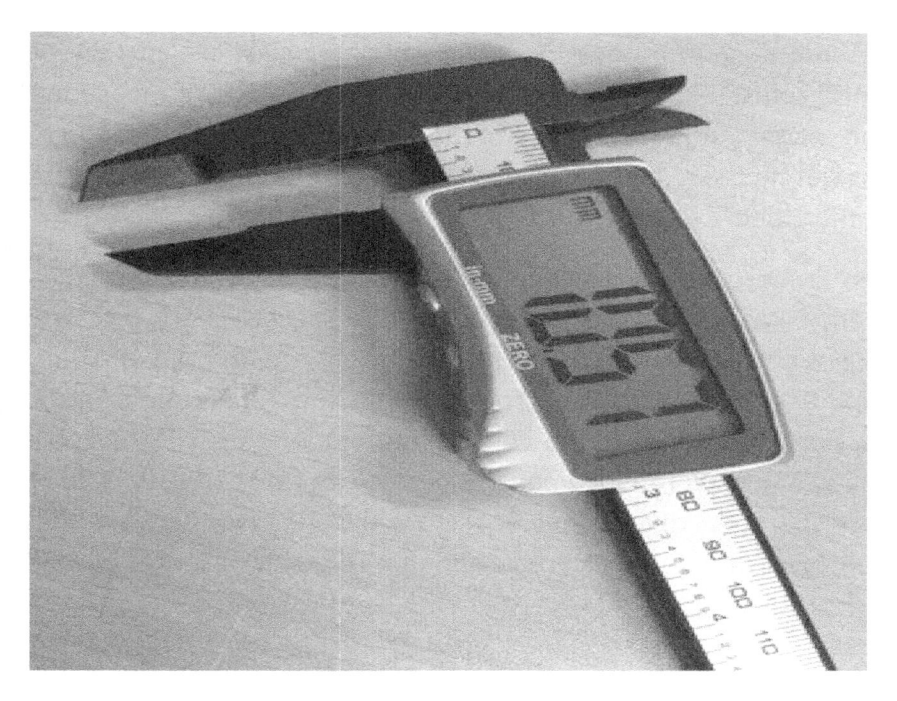

Conclusion

Embarking on the captivating journey of coin collecting comes with its own set of tools and supplies. It's like stepping into any hobby – you need the right gear to make the most of it. But fear not, fellow collectors, you don't have to assemble an arsenal of tools right from the start. Starting small is not just a piece of advice; it's a golden rule. A magnifier and a coin folder are your trusty companions as you take those initial steps into the world of coins. It's the simple joy of discovery, of observing the intricate details that make each coin unique.

As you progress in your coin-collecting adventure, so can your toolkit. Your collection will evolve, and so will your needs. Quality tools for documentation, handling, and storage become more critical as you introduce rarer and more valuable coins to your ensemble. Venturing into new territories, such as ancient or world coins, might lead you to appreciate the value of measuring and magnifying tools. These tools, like loyal guides, assist you in navigating the rich details of coins from different eras and corners of the globe.

Remember, the joy of coin collecting lies not just in the coins themselves but in the journey. So, feel free to start with the essentials, gradually adding tools that align with your growing expertise and collection. Your toolkit is a reflection of your passion, and as your coin collection blossoms, so will the tools you use to explore, document, and preserve these treasures. May your coin collecting journey be filled with curiosity, discovery, and the joy of finding that perfect addition to your collection. Happy collecting!

CHAPTER THREE: GETTING STARTED: SETTING UP YOUR COLLECTION

Embarking on the fascinating journey of coin collecting is like stepping into a time machine where each coin tells a story of history, politics, and culture. It's more than a hobby; it's a tangible exploration of our past, tucked into the metal crevices of each unique coin. In this chapter, we'll unravel the essentials of setting up your coin collection, ensuring that your initiation into this captivating world is not only rewarding but also infused with the joy of discovery.

3 Reasons to Start a Coin Collection

Why should you venture into the world of coin collecting? Well, besides the thrill of the hunt, there are three compelling reasons:

1. **Celebrate History**

Delve into the rich history etched on every coin, whether it's an ancient relic or a modern commemorative piece. Uncover the stories of political figures, royal figures, and the eras they represent.

2. **Make Money**

While it might not replace your day job, collecting valuable coins can be a profitable pursuit. Learn about unique coins and their values, potentially turning your hobby into a lucrative venture.

3. **Rise to the Challenge**

Coin collecting is not just about the coins; it's a journey filled with challenges and triumphs. Revel in the joy of discovering new coins through online platforms, antique stores, and beyond.

Common Collectible Coins and 5 Steps to Starting Your Coin Collection

Now that you're enticed, let's dive into the practicalities of coin collecting, starting with common collectible coins and a beginner-friendly roadmap.

Common Collectable Coins:

- The Lincoln Penny
- Walking Liberty Half Dollars
- 50 State quarters
- Coins with specific designs
- Coins from particular countries

5 Steps to Starting Your Coin Collection:

1. **Start Small with Your Coin Collection:** Dip your toes into coin collecting with accessible coins before taking the plunge. Research coin values, history, and grading, beginning with a coin type that ignites your interest.

2. **How to Store Your Coin Collection:** Master the art of proper coin storage to preserve their value and condition. Choose suitable containers like plastic holders, folders, or albums to prevent damage.

3. **How Are Coins Valued?** Understand the factors influencing coin values, including grade, preservation, and demand. Consider professional grading services like PCGS and NGC for accurate assessments.

4. **Start Hunting for Coins:** Explore your surroundings and online platforms for hidden treasures. Immerse yourself in the thrill of the hunt as you build your coin collection.

5. **Find Your Coin Collector Community:** Connect with fellow enthusiasts through online forums and local clubs. Attend events, share your passion, and expand your collection alongside a supportive community.

How to Sell Your Coin Collection and Coin Collecting at

Antique Malls

Ready to part with some coins or explore unique finds? Let's unravel the art of selling your collection and the wonders of antique malls.

How to Sell Your Coin Collection:

- Research online or consult experts to determine your collection's value.
- Approach local coin dealers, negotiate, and potentially turn your collection into a profitable endeavor.

Coin Collecting at Antique Malls:

- Move beyond online platforms and discover the charm of local antique malls.
- Engage with experts, hunt for bargains, and present your coins for evaluation in these unique settings.

Prepare to embark on your coin collecting journey armed with curiosity, knowledge, and a dash of adventure. This chapter aims to make the world of coin collecting not just accessible but downright enjoyable for collectors of all backgrounds.

Choosing Your Focus: Periods, Mint Marks, and Denominations

Hey there, fellow coin enthusiast! So, you've decided to dive into the fascinating world of coin collecting, and now you're faced with the exciting decision of choosing what coins to include in your budding treasure trove. Let's break down the nitty-gritty details to help you make the best choices for your collection.

1. Periods: Exploring Time Horizons

Recommendations:

- **Ancient Coins:** If you're a history buff, consider embarking on a journey through ancient civilizations. Collecting coins from

Greece, Rome, or other ancient cultures adds a touch of mystery and timelessness to your collection.

- **19th Century Coins:** Dive into the Victorian era or the American Civil War by gathering coins from the 1800s. These coins often carry historical significance and intricate designs, making them a favorite among collectors.

2. Mint Marks: The Secret Codes

Recommendations:

- **U.S. Mint Marks:** For American collectors, exploring U.S. mint marks can be thrilling. Look out for those from mints like Philadelphia (no mint mark), Denver (D), and San Francisco (S). Each carries its own story, and collecting them adds a geographical flair to your collection.

- **World Mint Marks:** If you're feeling a bit international, focus on coins from specific countries. The British Royal Mint (UK), the Royal Canadian Mint (Canada), and the Perth Mint (Australia) offer diverse and interesting coins.

3. Denominations: Counting the Coin Values

Profitable Denominations:

- **Gold Coins:** Historically, gold coins have shown good investment potential. Consider collecting gold coins from different periods and mints. They not only look stunning but can also increase in value over time.

Face Value and Quantity:

- **Pennies and Cents:** While pennies may not have a high face value individually, collecting them in quantity can be a fun and budget-friendly way to start. Plus, hunting for rare pennies is like searching for hidden treasures in your coin jar.

Specialized Focus for Readers:

- **For History Buffs:** If you love history, go deep into a specific historical period. Gather coins that circulated during significant events, turning your collection into a captivating history lesson.

- **For Geography Enthusiasts:** If you enjoy maps and geography, mint marks are your best friends. Collect coins from different mints worldwide, creating a diverse and visually appealing collection.

- **For Investors:** If you're looking at the investment side, consider focusing on gold coins and high-denomination coins. These have the potential to appreciate over time, making your collection not just a hobby but a smart investment.

Remember, your collection is your story, and the choices you make give it character. Whether you're drawn to the allure of ancient times, the mystery of mint marks, or the valuable face of gold coins, enjoy the journey of curating a collection that's uniquely yours.

CHAPTER FOUR: IDENTIFYING VALUABLE ERRORS IN POCKET CHANGE

Welcome to Chapter Four, where we're about to unravel the hidden treasures that might be jingling in your pocket change! Have you ever wondered if those coins you absentmindedly toss into your coin jar or wallet could be worth more than their face value? Well, you're in for a treat because we're delving into the captivating world of coin errors.

First things first, let's talk about what coin errors really are. Picture this: coins rolling off the minting press, and oops, something goes a bit haywire. That's where errors come into play. These are unexpected deviations from the standard manufacturing process and trust us; they can make a coin look quite different.

Now, why do these errors happen? Blame it on the complexities of the minting process. From misalignments to doubled images, the minting journey is rife with opportunities for unexpected twists. Even the slightest glitch can turn a regular coin into a unique specimen.

In this chapter, we're going to play detective and teach you how to spot those distinctive features that scream, "I'm an error coin!" From doubled dies to off-center strikes, we'll guide you through the maze of anomalies that can turn a common coin into a collector's gem.

Not all errors are created equal. Some are quirky but not necessarily valuable, while others can send collectors into a frenzy. We'll spill the beans on which error coins you should hold onto with a firm grip because they might just be your ticket to a little numismatic fortune.

So, whether you're a seasoned collector or just starting out, get ready to look at your pocket change in a whole new light. The coins you thought were ordinary might be hiding secret stories of minting mishaps and unexpected deviations. Let's embark on this coin-hunting adventure together and discover the hidden world of valuable errors!

Recognizing Common Errors

Ever found yourself squinting at a coin, wondering if it holds a hidden secret? Well, you're not alone. Identifying U.S. error coins might sound like a daunting task, but fear not! We're here to spill the beans on the specific features you should be on the lookout for.

1. Doubled Lettering or Design Features: The Telltale Signs

Imagine seeing double but on a coin! If you spot a doubling of letters, numbers, or any design details, you might have stumbled upon an error. Pay close attention to areas like the coin's date, inscriptions such as "IN GOD WE TRUST," "UNITED STATES OF AMERICA," or "E PLURIBUS UNUM," and significant parts of the design, like eyes, mouths, ears, or intricate hair details.

Now, not all doubled-up coins are errors, but here's the catch – the ones that are can be quite valuable. Keep an eye out for the elusive doubled die errors. These gems are born during the creation of the die, the tool that transforms blank coins into the currency we know. Some doubled die coins can fetch over $1,000!

A Quick Tip: Don't confuse doubled die errors with repunched mintmark errors. They might sound similar, but the devil's in the details. Doubled die errors happen during the die creation, while repunched mintmark errors occur when the letter punch leaves two impressions at different angles or locations.

2 – Off-Center Design: When Coins Dance to Their Own Beat

Ever noticed a coin that seems to be doing a little dance, with its design not quite centered? Well, that's not intentional, but it sure makes the coin stand out! When a coin is struck off-center, it's like a rebellious move during the minting process.

Spotting Off-Center Strikes: The Crescent Effect

Look closely, and you might see a crescent-shaped area of blank metal on the coin. It's a bit like the coin decided to shy away from the center stage. Also, keep an eye on the rim—the raised lip around the design. If it looks thicker on one side than the other, congratulations, you've got an off-center coin.

Guess what? These off-center coins might be common, but they're still considered errors. Don't let their commonality fool you—they're worth holding on to. In fact, the more drastic ones can even fetch you a cool $50 or more! Now, that's a pretty penny for a little minting mishap.

3 – Unusual Raised Straight or Squiggly Lines: The Coin's Artistic Flair

Coins aren't supposed to have random lines or markings, right? Well, when they do, it's like the coin is trying out a new artistic flair. But don't be too quick to dismiss these lines—they might be telling you a story of minting quirks.

Decoding Raised Lines: Polishing Marks vs. Die Breaks

Not all raised lines are created equal. Some are just there because of a little polishing, and these aren't exactly the coins that will make you jump for joy. But, and here's the exciting part, some raised lines are born from aging dies that decide to crack up a bit. These, my friend, are the valuable error coins you want to keep close.

Remember, if you spot a raised marking, hold onto that coin like it's a treasure map. Evaluate it further, and you might find yourself with a coin boasting a die crack or die break. The rarer ones in this category can be worth more than a handsome $100! Keep an eye out for those quirky BIE varieties on Lincoln cents—they're like the rockstars of die cracks, usually fetching $5 to $10.

4 – Missing Mintmarks, Numbers, or Letters: Coin's Mystery Makeover

Imagine finding a coin that seems to have forgotten a letter, number, or even its mint mark. It's like the coin went through a mystery makeover, shedding a few design elements along the way.

Deciphering Missing Details: Wear and Tear vs. Strikethrough Errors

Before you dismiss missing details as just wear and tear, consider this: sometimes, it's intentional, like a deliberate detail removal. But wait, there's more! If a foreign intruder (well, foreign matter) decides to gatecrash the minting process and obscures part of the design, you've got yourself a strikethrough error.

Hold onto those coins with missing elements, especially if it involves a little strikethrough drama. These coins can be more than a coin collector's dream—they can be worth a sweet $250 or more!

5 – Bubbles Or Raised Spots: Unraveling the Heat Mystery

Ever heard of coins taking a bubble bath in fire or dancing with a blowtorch? Well, strange as it may sound, some coins have faced the heat – literally! When exposed to intense heat, like a fire or a blowtorch, bubbles may appear on the surface. Die breaks can also create bubble-like bumps, known as die cuds.

If you stumble upon a coin with these peculiar bubbles or ripples, chances are it has a heated past. On copper-nickel clad coins, these bubbles might result from gases trapped between cladding layers. For pennies post-1982, tiny bubbles are often due to bonding imperfections between the outer copper layer and the zinc core.

Hold onto these bubbly coins! They might be worth $10 to $50, or perhaps even more. Don't be surprised if some die cracks mimic bubbles – these are known as die cuds and can fetch about $100 and up.

6 – Surface Areas That Have Peeled Away: Unmasking Lamination Errors

Coins can sometimes experience a wardrobe malfunction, with layers of metal peeling away due to imperfect chemical bonding during or after minting. If you spot a coin with missing metal layers, you might be onto a lamination error.

These quirky errors can be worth around $10 and up. Keep a keen eye for coins with peeled-off sections – they could be your ticket to a small numismatic windfall.

7 – The Wrong Color: Embracing the Odd Hues

Ever come across a silver penny or a coin flaunting hues that defy the norm? Hold onto it! That peculiar coloration might be a valuable error – specifically, a coin struck on the wrong metal, also known as a wrong planchet error.

To confirm its authenticity, get the coin professionally tested. These off-metal errors can be worth a pretty penny, sometimes $500 or more. Coins that break away from the expected color code are like hidden gems waiting to be discovered.

8 – The Wrong Size or Shape: When Coins Take a Walk on the Wild Side

Coins are like chameleons during minting mistakes – they might end up too big, too small, or even with peculiar shapes. A penny that appears gigantic or a misshapen quarter could be the result of minting mishaps like broadstrike, capped die, or clipped planchet errors.

Hold onto these peculiarly sized or shaped coins for further investigation. U.S. error coins in this category can be worth a cool $50 or more. It's a reminder that sometimes, the oddities are where the real value hides. So, if a coin seems to break the mold, let it break into your collection!

60

9 – Rim or Edge Oddities

Have you ever wondered why some coins look a bit off around the edges? Well, you might just be holding a treasure without realizing it. In this section, we're going to dive into the fascinating realm of rim and edge oddities – those little quirks that can turn an ordinary coin into something extraordinary.

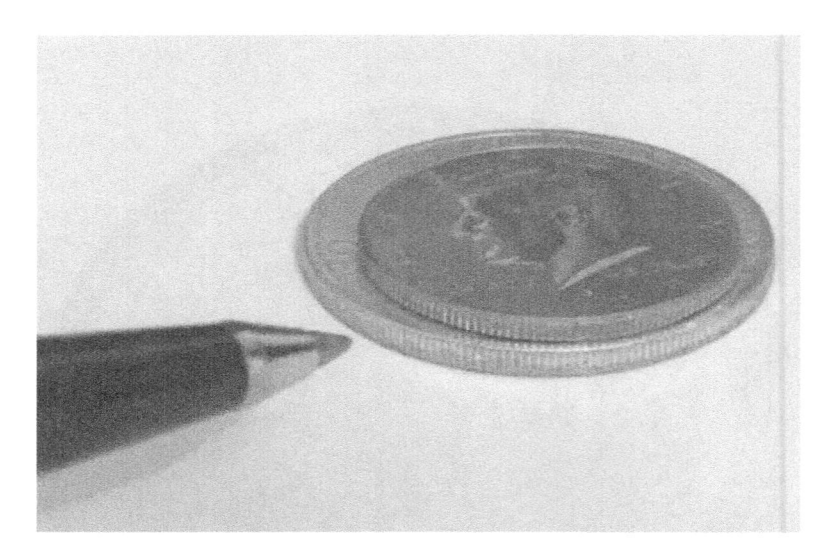

Decoding the Difference: Rim vs. Edge

Before we jump into the treasure hunt, let's get our terms straight. The rim is the raised part on both sides of the coin, creating a border, while the edge is the flat, outer part. Now, let's explore the different errors that can make these parts look, well, not quite right.

Common Rim Errors: A Closer Look

1. **Blank Coins:** Ever seen a coin with no design at all? That's a blank coin, and it's a charming error that can make your collection stand out.

2. **Broadstrikes:** Picture a coin that's a bit too wide for its own good. Broadstrikes happen when the coin isn't aligned correctly during the minting process, creating a broad, borderless look.

3. **Clipped Planchets:** Imagine a cookie with a bite taken out of it. Clipped planchets are coins with a part missing, making them a quirky addition to your collection.

4. **Die Cuds:** Sometimes, the minting dies get tired and leave a raised blob on the coin. These die cuds are like mini sculptures on your currency.

5. **Off-Center Coins:** Ever seen a coin where the design is hanging off the edge? That's an off-center coin, and it's an error that adds character.

Edge Errors: Uncovering the Unusual

1. **Missing Reeded Edges or Edge Lettering:** Keep an eye out for coins without those tiny vertical lines along the edge or missing letters. These omissions could turn your coin into a hidden gem.

2. **Orange Copper Stripe Missing:** If you spot a copper-nickel clad coin without its characteristic orange stripe on the outer edge, you might just be holding a unique find.

Hold On to the Oddities: Potential Value Awaits!

Remember, if you come across a coin with a peculiar edge or rim, don't be too quick to spend it. Take a moment to inspect it closely. If it turns out to be a genuine error, you could be looking at a coin worth a cool $100 or more! So, keep your eyes peeled for those weird-looking edges – they might just be your ticket to a numismatic jackpot.

Types of Coin Errors

Dive into the fascinating world of coin errors, where each misstep in the minting process creates a unique tale. Coin errors, often mistaken for mere misprints, are the intriguing outcomes of mistakes made right at the heart of the minting process. Let's unravel the mystery as we explore three distinct categories of these captivating anomalies.

1. Planchet Errors: Where Blanks Go Awry

Ever heard of a "planchet"? It's the blank canvas for coins, and errors in this category stem from its improper preparation. Imagine clipped planchets in peculiar shapes, planchets with the wrong thickness, or even blank planchets that missed their transformation. These are the quirks of the planchet error family, each telling a unique story of a coin's unconventional journey.

Visualize this: A quarter struck on the wrong planchet, creating a numismatic masterpiece of its own.

2. Die Errors: The Dance of Letters and Numbers

The minting dance involves dies, the maestros behind imparting letters, numbers, and images onto coins. One die takes the lead for the obverse, while another steps up for the reverse. If either encounters a hiccup, it leads to die errors—doubling of design elements or the captivating mismatch of two dies, creating the elusive "mule" coin.

Witness the intrigue: A Lincoln cent with a repunched mintmark, a testament to the dance of dies gone slightly offbeat.

3. Strike Errors: When Design Meets Coin Canvas

Picture the minting stage where designs are impressively stamped onto coins—the striking process. In this realm, errors manifest as off-center or misaligned strikes, designs finding their way onto the wrong-sized planchets, and other peculiar oddities.

Behold the spectacle: A 19th-century coin showcasing a brockage error, a striking example of design meeting coin canvas in an unexpected manner.

Remember, all these errors originate within the mint, unintentionally finding their way into circulation. This sets them apart from post-mint damage, ensuring that each error coin is a testament to the fascinating missteps in the art of minting. So, as you embark on your coin-collecting journey, keep an eye out for these unique stories etched into the very fabric of each coin's existence.

How to Spot Error Coins

Unraveling the Mystery: How to Spot Error Coins

Spotting error coins might sound like finding a needle in a haystack, but fear not – we've got the detective's guide to help you uncover these hidden treasures. While error coins are rare, they're not impossible to find. Here's your roadmap to becoming an error coin detective:

1. Batch Effect: Hunt in Numbers

Error coins often come in groups. The U.S. Mint produces coins in batches, so if there's a flaw or a miss-strike in one coin, it's likely that others in the same batch share the same peculiarity. Keep your eyes peeled for batches of coins that seem a bit out of the ordinary.

2. The Keen Eye Advantage: Observe the Unusual

Having a keen eye is your superpower. Sometimes, an error is obvious – a coin that just doesn't look like the others. But to truly master error spotting, familiarize yourself with famous error types. Some are like celebrities, easy to recognize, while others play the subtle game. A magnifying glass can be your sidekick for the more elusive errors.

3. Change Quest: Scrutinize Your Pocket Coins

Your everyday pocket change might hold secrets. Scrutinize those quarters, dimes, and pennies – you never know what might pop up. Look for anything that seems out of place, as even the smallest detail can turn a coin into a treasure.

4. Roll the Dice: Coin Rolls Unveil Surprises

Take a trip to your local bank and get yourself some coin rolls. It's like a treasure hunt and the best part? You won't lose money, even if your search turns up empty. Every coin in those rolls is worth exactly what you paid for it. It's a win-win!

5. Cherrypicking: The Art of Selecting

Feeling a bit more adventurous? Try cherrypicking. It's like flipping through a deck of cards, but with coins. Carefully inspect each one, whether it's from an estate sale or the bargain bin at your local coin shop. You might just pluck out a hidden gem.

Becoming an error coin detective requires patience, a dash of curiosity, and a willingness to explore. So, grab your magnifying glass and embark on this coin-hunting journey. Who knows what treasures you might uncover in the world of error coins!

Common Mint Error Coins

Welcome to the exciting world of Mint error coins, where imperfections turn into hidden treasures. In this chapter, we'll unravel the mysteries of some common Mint errors that might just be lurking in your pocket change.

1 – Doubled Die Error Coins

Imagine seeing double on your coin! Doubled dies are a popular type of error, where part of the coin image is duplicated. Mostly found in lettering, these errors can sometimes extend to the design itself. The famous 1955 doubled-die penny, valued at around $1,100, has been turning heads for over 50 years! While most doubled dies are worth $20 to $50, some can go even higher.

2 – Blank Planchet Error Coins

Spotting a blank planchet error is like finding a hidden canvas in your coins. These errors occur when a coin is struck on a blank piece of metal without any design. Easily distinguishable, these blanks can be worth a few dollars, with some fetching between $10 to $20.

3 – Broadstrike Error Coins

Broadstrike errors give your coins a unique twist. During the Minting process, if a coin isn't placed properly in the collar, it spreads out, creating an odd rim or no rim at all. The design may also be off-center. Depending on the coin type and the degree of over-width, these errors can be valued from $5 to over $200.

4 – Off-Center Error Coins

Off-center errors add an artistic touch to your collection. Some coins can be off by more than 50%, creating a unique half-and-half design. The more off-center, the higher the value. Prices vary widely, with many starting at $50 and climbing into the hundreds of dollars.

5 – Die Clash Error Coins

Die clashes reveal a clash of the titans among coin dies. When two dies clash without a coin in between, odd shapes appear on the coin's designs. Look for details from the opposing die impressed on one side. Even light die clashes can be worth $2 to $3, depending on the coin and the visible details.

6 – Repunched Mintmark Error Coins

Ever wondered why some pre-1990 coins seem to have a secret second mintmark hiding beneath the date? That's the magic of repunched mintmarks. Imagine the letter punch dancing on the coin at different angles, leaving not one but two impressions. Sometimes they overlap or touch, creating a doubling (or even tripling) effect. The value of these coins ranges from $3 to $15, depending on how dramatic the mintmark doubling is.

7 – Die Break / Die Crack Error Coins

As coin dies gracefully age, they might decide to crack or break apart. These defects show up as raised bumps, lines, or flat areas on the coin. While larger die breaks or cracks can fetch a pretty penny (pun intended), most are minor and not particularly valuable, ranging from $3 and up. It's like a coin's unique battle scar!

8 – Die Cud Error Coins

Picture a broad die break attached to the rim, resulting in a featureless metal blob extending from the rim inward. These are die cuds. Some are small and humble, worth very little, while others are grand, almost consuming the rim. Larger die cuds can bring in a handsome sum of $100 or more. It's like finding treasure on the edge of your coin!

9 – BIE Error Coins

A BIE error is like a secret code—a vertical die crack forming an "I" between the "B" and the "E" in the word Liberty on a penny. Often labeled as common mint error coins (or cherished varieties for diehard collectors), BIE pennies are worth a cool $3 to $5. It's a quirky addition to your penny collection!

10 – Clipped Planchet Error Coins

Ever seen a crescent-shaped coin and wondered how it got that way? Meet the clipped planchet error coins. During the coin-making process, the device cutting the planchets might get a bit too enthusiastic, resulting in crescent-shaped pieces. The value of these clipped coins varies from $5 to $100, depending on factors like coin type, grade, and the amount of missing metal. A unique twist to your coin collection indeed!

So, there you have it—common mint errors that not only make your collection stand out but can also bring unexpected value

Rare Mint Error Coins

In the enchanting realm of coin collecting, there exists a captivating category of treasures known as mint error coins. These peculiar coins, marked by unexpected deviations from the standard minting process, hold both rarity and value for avid collectors. Let's delve into some of these fascinating mint errors that elevate numismatic pursuits to a thrilling treasure hunt.

Brockage Error Coins

Imagine a coin getting stuck to a die after being struck, leaving a mirror image imprinted on subsequent planchets. These mesmerizing brockage errors, with their negative, mirror-like impressions, are both unique and scarce. Even modern brockage pennies, nickels, dimes, and quarters can fetch around $75 and more, making them a captivating find for collectors. Older brockage errors or those on larger denominations hold even greater value, adding an extra layer of allure to your collection.

Die Cap Error Coins: When Coins Transform Into Caps

Remember the brockage error? Well, when that coin becomes stuck to the die, it creates another captivating error known as a capped die. This misshapen coin, resembling a bottle cap, is a remarkable and relatively rare mint error worth approximately $150 and above. Each die cap coin narrates a unique story of its journey through the minting process, making it a distinctive addition to your collection.

Waffled / Cancelled Error Coins: Mutilation Transforms Into Collectibles

When the U.S. Mint identifies an error, it undergoes a fascinating process called waffling, resulting in coins with distinct ridges and crevices. These waffled coins, born out of minting mishaps, date back to around 2003 and are worth approximately $20 and beyond. Their peculiar appearance, a result of the mint's effort to cancel errors, adds an intriguing chapter to your collection.

Die Trial Error Coins: Testing the Minting Waters

U.S. Mint officials, meticulous in their craft, conduct die trials to test the strength of the die strike and other striking process aspects. Die trial error coins, displaying light design details or striking abnormalities, are rare finds and can be valued at $250 or more. These coins bear witness to the meticulous testing that goes into minting, adding a touch of exclusivity to your collection.

Double Denomination Error Coins: A Curious Coin Crossover

Picture a coin returning to the press, only to be struck by dies from a different denomination. This whimsical mishap results in a double denomination error, a rarity both curious and valuable. With values starting at $250, these coins spark fascination, prompting collectors to ponder the incredible journey that led to such an extraordinary minting error.

Lamination Error Coins: Unveiling Surface Anomalies

Planchets suffering from surface maladies like dirt, grease, or gas bubbles result in lamination errors. While minor lamination errors may not command high values, major laminations, especially on clad coins, can be worth a considerable sum. Small lamination errors fetch $5 to

$10, while major ones can reach $25 to $50 or more, adding diversity to your collection.

Multiple Strike Error Coins: A Symphony of Impressions

Occasionally, coins undergo multiple strikes on the press, showcasing multiple impressions of the design. These rare errors, distinct from doubled dies, are valued starting at around $50. The unique patterns created by multiple strikes make these coins a captivating find for collectors with an eye for the extraordinary.

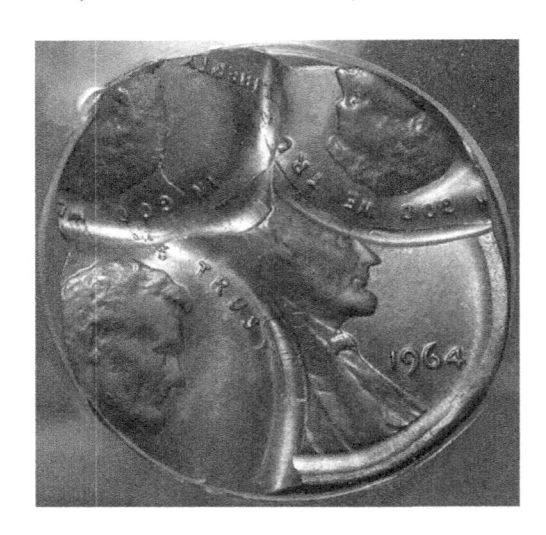

20th Century Variety/Type Identifier Codes

ADO = Abraded Die Obverse

ADR = Abraded Die Reverse

BIE = Die break between the letters of LIBERTY

CUD	=	Major die break
DDO	=	Doubled Die Obverse
DDR	=	Doubled Die Reverse
DGO	=	Die Gouge Obverse
DGR	=	Die Gouge Reverse
IMM	=	Inverted MintMark
MDO	=	Master die Doubled Obverse
MDR	=	Master die Doubled Reverse
MMO	=	MintMark Omission
MMP	=	MintMark Placement
MMS	=	MintMark Style
MPD	=	MisPlaced Date
ODV	=	Obverse Design Variety
OMM	=	Over MintMark
RDV	=	Reverse Design Variety
RED	=	Re-Engraved Design
ROT	=	ROTated dies
RPD	=	RePunched Date
RPM	=	RePunched Mintmark
SDO	=	Series hub Doubled Obverse
SDR	=	Series hub Doubled Reverse
WHO	=	Working Hub doubled Obverse

WHR = Working Hub doubled Reverse

CHAPTER FIVE: BUILDING YOUR COLLECTION FROM SCRATCH

Welcome to the captivating world of coin collecting, a hobby that bridges the past and present, offering enthusiasts a tangible connection to history. Whether you're a seasoned collector or a newcomer, the allure of coins lies in their beauty, rarity, and the intriguing stories they carry about politics, history, and society.

Coins, much like masterpieces from Classical Antiquity and the Renaissance, hold a unique place in the hearts of collectors. Unlike monumental sculptures or paintings, coins are remarkably accessible, allowing anyone to own a piece of historical significance. Throughout history, coins have been cherished as gifts and symbols of good luck during special occasions, a tradition that echoes into the present day.

As you embark on the journey of collecting and studying coins, you'll discover fascinating iconographical trends. The earliest coins influenced the standardized depictions of deities, rulers, and personifications that we recognize in the currency we use today. Coins, especially those from the Roman Empire, served as messengers of political messages, conveying military conquests, dynastic changes, and architectural marvels to citizens across vast geographical distances.

Starting a coin collection may initially seem daunting, given the myriad themes, metals, eras, and thousands of years of history to explore. However, coin collecting is surprisingly accessible and budget-friendly. Consider the coins in your pocket—there are approximately 29 billion coins in circulation in the UK alone. Your spare change could be the starting point for your collection.

For instance, did you know that there are over 30 different £2 coin designs in circulation? Some have mintages in the hundreds of millions, while others are as low as 500,000. By studying your spare change and gathering diverse £2 coin designs, you can kickstart your coin collection. Imagine the pride of including a rare gem like the 2002 Commonwealth Games (Ireland) £2 coin in your collection.

Numismatic collections can be tailored based on personal preferences, be it historical periods, depicted personalities, mythology, natural history, or politics. Each coin collection holds a unique meaning for its collector, making it a deeply personal endeavor. As you begin your journey into the realm of coin collecting, consider a few essential points that will enrich your experience and make your collection truly yours.

Budgeting for Coin Collecting: Tips for Beginners

1. Start Simple and Small: Unless you're a millionaire, it's wise to ease into the hobby. Begin with smaller coin purchases and sets that are easy to assemble. For example, many successful collectors started with sets of Lincoln pennies. These coins are still in circulation and can be purchased at coin shows, shops, or online for a moderate price.

2. Collect What You Like: The key to a fulfilling collection is to collect what interests you. Whether it's a fascinating design, historical significance, or a captivating story associated with the coin, choose coins that pique your interest. Research the history of the coins you collect, but be cautious when making online purchases to avoid overpricing or counterfeits.

3. Handle Coins Carefully & Store Them Properly: Despite being made of metal, the delicate surface of a coin can be easily damaged. Use cotton or latex gloves when handling coins, or touch them only by the edges. Never clean a coin, as this can reduce its value. Proper storage and handling techniques ensure the longevity and value of your coin collection.

4. It's Not a Race: Building a valuable coin collection takes time. Rushing into purchases often leads to frustration and potential financial losses when selling. Take the time to learn about the coins you're interested in before making a purchase. Patience is key, and coin collecting is a hobby that can last a lifetime.

5. Connect with a Reputable Dealer: Seek guidance from a trusted numismatic expert. In London, a hub of numismatic activity, you can find dealers with decades of experience. Look for dealers affiliated with internationally acclaimed trade associations like IAPN, BNTA (in the UK), or ANA (for USA-based dealers). Membership in these associations signifies a commitment to customer care and due diligence.

6. Magazines and Websites: Explore coin collecting magazines like Coin World and Numismatic News for valuable information. Online resources can be beneficial, but be cautious of websites that focus more on selling coins than providing genuine information.

7. Join a Coin Club: Being part of a coin club provides opportunities to learn more about coins and stay engaged in the hobby. Search for local coin clubs or consider joining the American Numismatic Association (ANA). Specialty coin clubs cater to various interests and expertise levels.

8. Visit a Coin Show or Coin Shop: Online purchases lack the tactile experience of holding and inspecting coins. Attend coin shows or visit local coin shops to evaluate coins firsthand before purchasing. Trusted coin dealers can offer valuable insights, and some shows may include seminars for new collectors.

9. Have a Plan: Before starting a coin collection, research the cost involved and create a plan. Set up a spreadsheet listing the coins you need, their estimated costs, and desired grades. This helps you stay organized, avoid duplicate purchases, and plan your budget accordingly. If there are expensive coins you aspire to own, consider saving up for them over time.

10. Connect with a Reputable Dealer: Seek guidance from a trusted numismatic expert. In London, a hub of numismatic activity, you can find dealers with decades of experience. Look for dealers affiliated with internationally acclaimed trade associations like IAPN, BNTA (in the UK), or ANA (for USA-based dealers). Membership in these associations signifies a commitment to customer care and due diligence.

11. Ensure Authenticity: Opt for dealers who guarantee the authenticity of the coins they sell. Reputable dealers should readily provide a certificate of authenticity upon request. The certificate should detail essential information about the coin, including its description, metal type, reference, weight, and provenance.

12. Mind the Condition: Condition significantly influences a coin's value. Inquire about any potential repairs, cleaning, or other alterations. Be especially vigilant when buying online. Check for signs of wear, mounting traces, scratches, or residues. Different metals, like gold and silver, require distinct care.

CHAPTER SIX: CONNECTING WITH THE COIN COLLECTING COMMUNITY

In almost every city, there's a hidden world of enthusiasts passionate about collecting coins. Joining coin clubs or associations is not just for seasoned collectors—it's an open invitation, especially for beginners or those with curious kids. Here's a breakdown of why you should consider becoming part of a coin community:

Most cities host local coin clubs or associations. Joining is straightforward, often requiring a minimal fee, sometimes as low as $20. These fees help cover club activities and resources. Local clubs typically hold frequent meetings, at least once a month. This offers a chance to regularly connect with fellow collectors.

Explore and join coin clubs through platforms like *htts://www.coinlink.com/directory/clubs.html* and *http://collectingclubs.com/*. These links provide gateways to various clubs, making it easy to find one that suits your preferences.

Benefits of Joining:

- **Knowledge Sharing:** Coin clubs are a treasure trove of information. Seasoned collectors often share their expertise, offering valuable insights to beginners.

- **Networking:** Connect with like-minded individuals, from novices to seasoned numismatists. Exchange tips, stories, and maybe even coins! Members have vast experience you can tap from.

- **Access to Resources:** Clubs often have collective resources. You might gain access to reference materials, specialized tools, or even discounts from affiliated dealers.

- **Events and Exhibitions:** Stay updated on coin-related events, exhibitions, and fairs. Clubs frequently organize or participate in these gatherings.

- You can buy coins from members through auctions.
- It is also an avenue for kids to learn.

For an even broader connection, explore *http://www.coincommunity.com/dictionary/*. It's not just a dictionary; it's a gateway to a vibrant online community. It allows you to access forums, discussions, and a wealth of information. Imagine a coin club as a gathering of people who share a common love for collecting coins. Some focus on a local level, while others span entire countries. They're places to talk, share, and revel in the joy of coin collecting.

Joining Clubs and Associations

Let's explore the numerous benefits of joining national numismatic organizations. These clubs not only offer engaging activities and events but also provide valuable services to members. In this overview, we'll focus on major organizations at the national level, each catering to specific interests within the diverse world of numismatics.

American Numismatic Association (ANA)

Annual membership fee: $30 (Gold), $46 (Platinum). Benefits include access to the World's Fair of Money and National Money Show, Virtual Money Museum Exhibits, educational programs, free entry to ANA coin shows, and a subscription to The Numismatist. Gold and Platinum memberships offer additional perks, and special Youth Memberships are available for $16 and $36.

More information: *https://www.money.org/*.

American Numismatic Society (ANS)

Annual membership fees range from $115 to $215, with a discounted student membership available. Membership includes subscriptions to ANS publications, access to the extensive library and collection in New York City, and discounted enrollment in ANS Lyceum courses. Weekly Long Table lectures and seminars provide exclusive educational content for members.

More information: **https://numismatics.org/**.

Colonial Coin Collectors Club (C4)

Annual membership fee: $31 (adults), $11 (under 18). It focuses on pre-Federal American colonial coinage, offering newsletters, access to a lending library, and an annual convention featuring educational presentations and study groups.

More information: **https://colonialcoins.org/**.

Liberty Seated Collectors Club (LSCC)

Annual membership fee: $30. Benefits include print issues of the Gobrecht Journal, the monthly E-Gobrecht, access to a community of

Seated Liberty collectors, and educational programs at regional and national coin shows. Members also receive a free CAC membership.

More information: **http://www.lsccweb.org/**.

Ancient Coin Collectors Guild (ACCG)

It's a Non-profit organization focusing on ancient coin collecting and advocacy. Membership fees contribute to educational efforts and lobbying against import restrictions on ancient coins. It offers extensive information on current import restrictions and advocacy work.

More information: **https://accguild.org/**.

Medal Collectors of America

Annual membership fee: $80 (quarterly hardcopy editions) or $40 (electronic editions). It focuses on the study and collection of artistic and historical medals, hosting annual meetings, seminars, and offering research support.

More information: **https://www.medalcollectors.org/**.

Numismatic Literary Guild (NLG)

Open to numismatic authors, publishers, and editors. It provides access to a monthly newsletter, Writer's Competition, and an annual gala.

More information: **https://www.nlgonline.org/**.

American Israel Numismatic Association (AINA)

Annual membership fee: $18 (digital), $40 (print), and $10 for youth members (10 to 19 years old). Members receive the quarterly magazine "The Shekel," access to digital annual member meetings, and the opportunity to compete for "The Shekel" prize. New members receive a challenge coin celebrating the 100th anniversary of women's suffrage in the US.

More information: **https://www.theshekel.org/index.php**.

While this list is not exhaustive, these organizations offer a diverse range of opportunities for numismatists to engage, learn, and connect with like-minded enthusiasts. Joining a club or association is not just about collecting coins; it's about becoming part of a vibrant community that shares your passion for numismatics.

CHAPTER SEVEN: CARING FOR YOUR COLLECTION
Proper Handling and Storage Techniques

Coins are more than just currency; they are tiny masterpieces that hold a piece of history in their metal embrace. As guardians of these small works of art, coin collectors play a crucial role in preserving not only their financial value but also the stories and historical significance engraved on each coin. Proper coin conservation and care are essential to safeguard their value, beauty, and the narratives they carry through time.

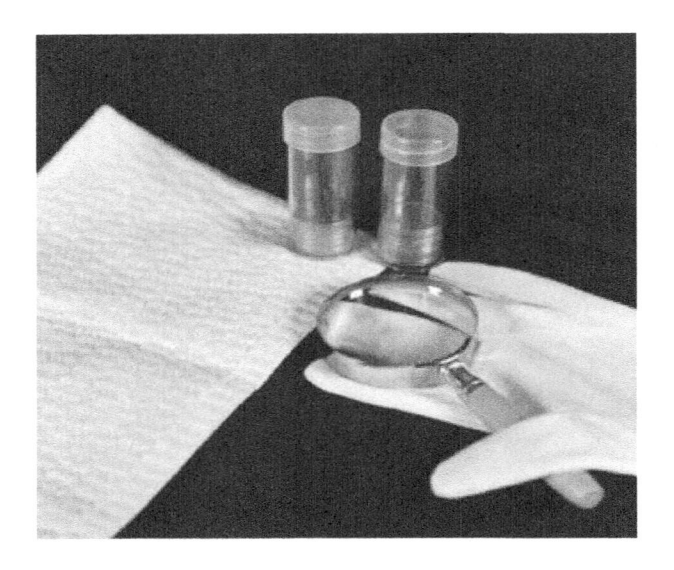

Clean Hands, White Gloves

The cardinal rule of coin preservation begins with clean hands. Treat coins like the precious jewels they are; avoid touching the surface with bare hands to prevent leaving fingerprints or transferring dirt. In Chapter Two, we emphasized the exceptional practice of wearing white gloves, ensuring an added layer of protection during handling.

Touching coins with bare hands can lead to corrosion over time, diminishing their aesthetic and historical value.

Avoiding Corrosive Materials

Coins are sensitive to their environment, and contact with corrosive materials can have detrimental effects. Handle coins in an environment free from substances like acidic or corrosive chemicals. The chemicals from everyday items, such as cleaning solutions, can tarnish coins and impact their condition. Exercise caution and keep coins away from potential contaminants.

Vigilant Monitoring

The responsibility of a coin collector goes beyond acquisition; it extends to vigilant monitoring. Regularly inspect coins for any signs of degradation. Early detection allows for timely intervention, preserving the coin's condition. Like curators in a museum, collectors must actively ensure the well-being of their numismatic treasures.

Respect for Art and History

Properly preserving coins is an act of respect for art and history. Each coin encapsulates a moment in time, a story waiting to be told. By handling and storing them with care, collectors honor the craftsmanship and historical significance these small marvels represent.

Environmental Considerations

Preserving coins extends beyond their physical handling; it involves creating an ideal storage environment. Temperature fluctuations and humidity levels can adversely affect the condition of coins, leading to oxidation and stains. A clean and stable environment is crucial for the long-term preservation of numismatic treasures.

Controversy Surrounding Preservation

Coin preservation often sparks controversy among collectors. The golden rule here is: do not clean coins. Cleaning, if done improperly, can cause irreversible damage, stripping away the patina that adds character and history to the coin. If a coin appears excessively dirty or tarnished, it's advisable to consult a conservation expert for guidance on appropriate cleaning methods.

Individual Storage

To further ensure the well-being of each coin, store them individually. This prevents coins from coming into contact with each other, reducing the risk of scratches, abrasions, or reactions between different metals. Individual storage also simplifies the monitoring process, allowing collectors to assess the condition of each coin without interference.

Handling Your Collection

1. **Hold Coins by the Edges:** Use soft cotton gloves or hold the coin by its edges between your thumb and forefinger. Do this over a soft towel or surface to prevent damage if the coin is dropped.

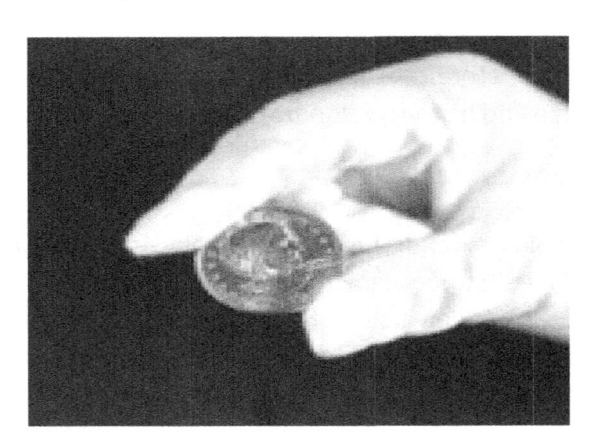

2. **Avoid Polishing:** Resist the temptation to polish your coins excessively. Polishing can reduce a coin's value, and collectors often prefer older coins with natural age coloration. If cleaning is necessary, use mild soap and water. Pat the coin dry with a soft towel; avoid brushing or rubbing, as it can scratch the delicate surface.

Storing Your Collection

1. **Keep Coins Cool and Dry:** Sharp changes in temperature and moisture can lead to discoloration that devalues coins. Avoid talking directly over coins to prevent tiny droplets of saliva, which can create spots difficult to remove.

2. **Use Original Holders:** Modern coin sets and individual coins should be bought and sold in their original cases and capsules. The Mint provides protective plastic cases called lenses or folders for coin sets. Individual coins come in capsules fitted into folders or boxes. Consider other storage options like 2" x 2" cardboard or plastic holders, plastic tubes, capsules, sleeves, envelopes, or albums.

3. **Choose Appropriate Holders:** For high-value coins, opt for hard plastic holders. Professional coin grading services use sealed holders called slabs to protect authenticated and graded coins.

4. **Use Acid-Free Materials:** Utilize acid-free cardboard and plastic holders that are free from polyvinyl chloride (PVC). Acid and PVC can damage a coin's surface over time, with PVC eventually coating it with a sticky green slime.

In conclusion, coin preservation is a meticulous and multifaceted practice. It involves not only the careful handling of these miniature treasures but also the creating of environment that safeguards their integrity. By approaching coin preservation with the reverence it deserves, collectors become stewards of history, ensuring that these small artifacts endure for generations to come.

CHAPTER EIGHT: GRADING YOUR COINS: A BEGINNER'S GUIDE

Welcome to the fascinating world of coin grading! Ever wondered why some coins look shinier and more pristine than others, even if they're of the same denomination? Well, the answer lies in the concept of coin grading.

Coin grading is the process of evaluating a coin's condition, and determining the extent of wear and tear it has experienced over time. Just like anything we use daily, coins, too, show signs of aging. Think about the pennies, nickels, dimes, and quarters you handle regularly – have you noticed some looking more worn than others?

Now, here's a question: have you ever wondered how collectors assess and rank these coins for their condition and value?

In this guide, we'll delve into the world of coin grading, demystifying the process for beginners like you. One influential system we'll explore is the Dr. William Sheldon Grading System, developed in 1949. This system, widely used by collectors, provides a structured way to grade and rank coins, helping enthusiasts like you understand not only the condition of your coins but also their market value.

So, buckle up as we embark on this journey of understanding how to assess, grade, and appreciate the unique qualities of your coin collection!

What Is Coin Grading?

At its core, coin grading is the process of determining a coin's physical condition and, consequently, its market value. It requires a keen eye, years of experience, and a profound understanding of the nuances that make each coin unique. Grading involves evaluating specific variables, including eye appeal, wear, mint state, strength of strike, major features, rarity, and luster.

The grading scale ranges from one to 70, with higher grades indicating better condition. A perfect coin receives a grade of 70. However, grading is more art than science, demanding extensive knowledge. Even the slightest imperfections can significantly impact a coin's value, turning a seemingly ordinary piece into a valuable collectible worth hundreds or even thousands of dollars.

Understanding the Purpose of Coin Grading

The primary purpose of coin grading is twofold: to assess a coin's physical condition accurately and to establish its market value. Grading involves evaluating specific variables, including:

1. **Eye Appeal:** The overall visual attractiveness of the coin.
2. **Contact Marks:** Any blemishes or scratches resulting from handling.
3. **Wear:** The extent to which the coin's surface has been worn down.
4. **Mint State:** Whether the coin is circulated or uncirculated.
5. **Strength of Strike:** The sharpness and clarity of the coin's design.
6. **Major Features:** The prominence of significant design elements.
7. **Rarity:** The scarcity of the coin.
8. **Luster:** The coin's sheen or shine.

The grading scale is a numerical system ranging from one to 70, with higher numbers signifying better conditions. A grade of 70 represents a flawless, perfect coin.

Carlos Clifton

Common Coin Grades

1. **Poor (P-1):** Damaged and barely identifiable.
2. **Very Good (VG-8):** Generally dull and worn with noticeable contact marks.
3. **Very Fine (VF-20):** Acceptable with moderate wear; essential details are still visible.
4. **Extremely Fine (EF-40):** Shows light wear, with clear finer details.
5. **About Uncirculated (AU-50):** Light wear on the highest points; acceptable eye appeal.
6. **Mint State Basal (MS-60):** Uncirculated but with no attractive eye appeal.
7. **Mint State Acceptable (MS-63):** Uncirculated with small contact marks and average strike.
8. **Mint State Choice (MS-65):** Uncirculated with attractive high quality and minimal contact marks.
9. **Mint State Perfect (MS-70):** A flawless coin with original luster and a sharp strike.

History of Coin Grading

In the early days of coin collecting, grading was subjective, with only two terms: new and used. As numismatics gained popularity, the need for a standardized grading system became evident. In 1948, Dr. William Sheldon introduced the Sheldon Coin Grading Scale, a revolutionary system that transformed the world of coin grading.

The Sheldon Coin Grading Scale

The Sheldon Scale, ranging from one to 70, is the industry standard for coin grading. A grade of 70 signifies a perfect, uncirculated coin with flawless eye appeal. Uncirculated coins, free from wear and tear, are the only ones that can achieve this pinnacle grade. The scale includes mini-scales for uncirculated coins (Mint State or MS), about uncirculated coins (AU), and circulated coins.

Navigating the Sheldon Scale

- **Uncirculated Coins (Mint State or MS):** Grades range from MS-60 (Basal) to MS-70 (Perfect).

- **About Uncirculated Coins (AU):** Grades include AU-50, showing light wear, to AU-58, nearing uncirculated condition.

- **Circulated Coins:** The most common coin type, ranging from P-1 (poor) to EF-49 (Extremely Fine).

How to Grade Coins: Step-by-Step

Coin grading is an essential skill for any collector, providing a standardized method to assess a coin's condition and value. Whether you're new to coin collecting or looking to refine your grading skills, this step-by-step guide will walk you through the process with clarity and detail.

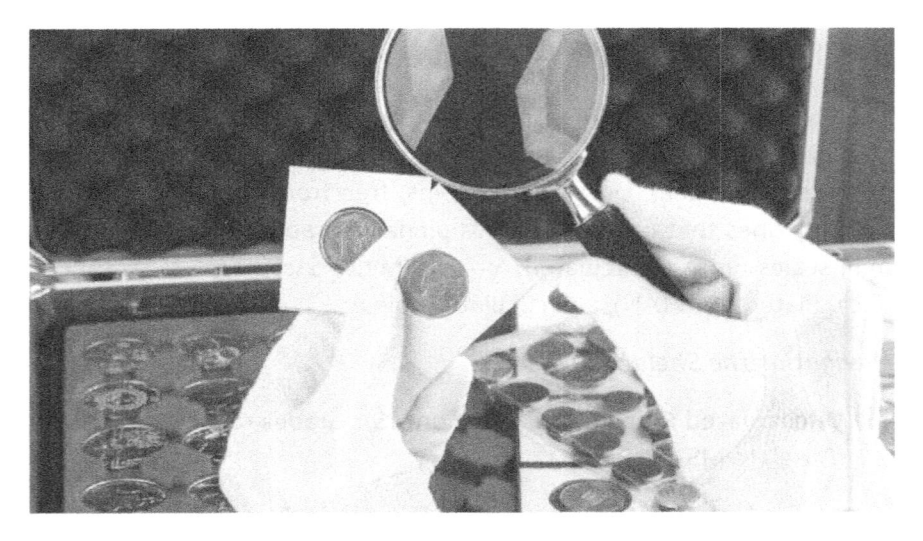

Step One: Set the Stage

Begin your grading process in a well-lit environment with a bright light source of at least 75 watts. Maintain a one-foot distance between the coin and the light to ensure optimal visibility. Gently hold the coin by its edges, using your thumb and index finger. This minimizes the risk of introducing fingerprints or damage during the grading process.

Step Two: Magnify the Details

To properly evaluate the coin, employ a magnifier or jeweler's loupe with a 6x to 8x magnification. This tool allows you to scrutinize the coin's date, major design elements, mint marks, bag marks, scuff marks, and overall design. Note the coin's color—whether it's original, darkened, or lightly toned—and assess its luster, categorizing it as poor, fine, or possessing average shine.

Step Three: Evaluate Major Features

Examine the coin's major features and determine its condition based on established scales. For instance, does it exhibit slight wear on high points with minimal contact marks? This could classify it as "About Uncirculated." If there's no wear, it falls under the "Uncirculated" or mint state category. The "Circulated State" encompasses coins with visible wear, scuff marks, contact marks, striking defects, or moderate damage.

Step Four: Observe Finer Details

While gently holding the coin, rotate it to observe finer details such as hairlines, small rim nicks, and contact marks. Ask yourself:

- Does the coin possess appealing eye appeal?
- Is it lightly worn?
- Does it retain its original mint luster?
- Are there detracting scuff marks?

Precision is crucial in this assessment.

Step Five: Refer to the Sheldon Scale

Compare the coin's overall condition to the Sheldon Scale, which provides a standardized grading system. Consider the coin's features, but avoid obsessing over micro-details that may lead to inaccurate grading.

How Do You Know if Your Coins Are Worth Grading?

Before investing in grading services, evaluate the potential return on investment (ROI). Consider factors like shipping costs, grading fees, turnaround time, and insurance. Generally, common-date coins, unless in Mint State condition, and type coins without AU+ condition or mid-1800s or earlier mintage, may not warrant grading. For instance, a 2000 Lincoln Cent in MS-68 might be worth $80, but with an MS-70 grade, it could fetch over $2,000.

Top Coin Grading Companies

When it comes to grading coins, four major players stand out in the United States. These companies, accredited by the Third Party Grading Database (TPG), are the go-to choices for coin dealers and collectors worldwide.

1. Professional Coin Grading Service (PCGS)

PCGS, the world leader in numismatics, sets the standard for coin grading. Their services include Tru-View high-definition coin photography, setting them apart in the industry. PCGS offers various grading tiers:

- **Silver Tier:** $69/year
- **Gold Tier:** $149/year (includes four grading vouchers)
- **Platinum Tier:** $249/year (includes eight grading vouchers)

2. Numismatic Guaranty Corporation (NGC)

NGC, the largest grading organization in terms of volume, is endorsed by the American Numismatic Association (ANA). Notably, NGC doesn't grade coins with any modifications. Membership options for NGC include:

- **Free Membership**
- **Associate Membership:** $25/year
- **Premium Membership:** $149/year (includes $150 NGC credit)
- **Elite Membership:** $299/year (includes $150 NGC credit and bulk discounts)

3. Independent Coin Graders (ICG)

ICG focuses solely on grading services and is distinguished by significantly lower fees compared to PCGS and NGC. They provide a cost-effective option for collectors seeking reliable grading.

4. American Numismatic Association Certification Service (ANACS)

As the oldest service for United States coins, ANACS boasts a rich history, certifying extremely rare coins, tokens, and metals since 1972.

How Much Does it Cost to Get a Coin Graded?

Understanding the cost of getting your coin graded involves considering both membership fees and individual grading charges. Let's break down the expenses associated with the top two professional grading companies in the U.S.

PCGS Membership Fees:

- **Silver Tier:** $69/year
- **Gold Tier:** $149/year (four grading vouchers)
- **Platinum Tier:** $249/year (eight grading vouchers)

These membership fees don't cover the individual cost of grading each coin you submit, which varies based on the coin type and maximum value. Individual grading charges typically range from $5 to $65.

NGC Membership Fees:

- **Free Membership**
- **Associate Membership:** $25/year
- **Premium Membership:** $149/year (includes $150 NGC credit)
- **Elite Membership:** $299/year (includes $150 NGC credit and bulk discounts)

Similar to PCGS, individual grading charges are separate and depend on factors such as coin type and maximum value, with fees ranging from $5 to $65.

Conclusion

Choosing the right coin grading company and understanding the associated costs are crucial steps in the world of numismatics. Whether you opt for the prestige of PCGS, the volume of NGC, the affordability of ICG, or the historical significance of ANACS, each company brings its unique value to the table. As you embark on your coin grading journey, consider your collecting goals, budget, and the specific attributes of your coins. Get ready to elevate your coin collecting experience with the assurance and certification provided by these esteemed grading companies!

CHAPTER NINE: UNDERSTANDING MARKET VALUES

So, you've delved into the intriguing universe of error coins, those unique treasures that bear unexpected quirks and deviations. Now, as you contemplate parting ways with some of these distinctive pieces or diving into the world of trading, a few crucial steps can make the process smoother and more rewarding.

Before you embark on the journey of selling or trading your error coins, it's paramount to discern the types of errors that hold a special allure for potential buyers. Errors can range from minting mistakes to anomalies in design or metal composition. To make informed decisions, consider enlisting the expertise of renowned grading services like PCGS (Professional Coin Grading Service) or NGC (Numismatic Guaranty Company). These seasoned professionals not only authenticate your coins but also provide insights into the specific errors that may attract more buyers.

Having your error coins authenticated by experts serves a dual purpose. Firstly, it assures potential buyers of the legitimacy and uniqueness of your coins, instilling confidence in their purchase. Secondly, it sets a standard for evaluating the value of your error coins, offering a benchmark that resonates within the coin collecting community.

Understanding the value of your error coins is a pivotal aspect of the selling and trading process. The worth of these intriguing pieces is influenced by various factors, including their condition, rarity, and what a buyer is willing to pay for them. To navigate this terrain effectively, delve into research or consult experts to gauge the market demand for specific error types.

How to Sell and Trade Error Coins

So, you've curated an impressive collection of coins, perhaps stumbled upon an error gem or two, and now you find yourself at the crossroads of deciding whether to part with some or all of your cherished treasures. Whether driven by a desire to upgrade, refocus your collection, or explore new avenues, the decision to sell or trade coins is a significant one. This comprehensive guide aims to demystify the process, providing you with a roadmap to navigate the various options available for selling or trading error coins. Let's embark on this journey, weighing the pros and cons of each avenue, and empowering you to make informed decisions about your numismatic assets.

Local Dealers: Your Friendly Neighborhood Connection

The journey to sell or trade your error coins can begin right in your local community – with coin dealers. These individuals are not just aficionados but are also in the business of acquiring unique coins. Visiting a local dealer offers a straightforward transaction – bring in your coins, get a fair assessment, and walk away with cash in hand. The convenience is undeniable, with no shipping hassles or minimum value requirements.

However, it's crucial to manage expectations. Local dealers, while convenient, might not offer the highest possible price for your coins. They have their profit margins to consider when reselling to other customers. For a seamless experience, it's advisable to research and choose a reputable dealer. Consider leveraging relationships with dealers you've worked with before.

Coin Shows: Where Opportunities Unfold

If you're open to a more dynamic selling experience, coin shows could be your stage. Whether it's a small local event or a grand gathering like the *ANA's National Money Show or World's Fair of Money*, these shows attract a diverse array of dealers. Bringing your error coins to a show allows you to explore multiple offers from different dealers.

The process involves shopping your collection around, gauging interest, and collecting offers. Once you've gathered a few proposals, you can compare and return to the dealer who presented the most enticing offer. This approach, while potentially fetching higher prices than local dealers, does come with its own set of considerations. Traveling to shows, especially those located far away, can be a logistical challenge.

Coin Auctions: Bidding for Success

For those seeking an exciting selling experience, coin auctions offer a platform where buyers compete for your error coins. Participating in a well-known auction house or online auction event can generate significant interest. The competitive bidding process often results in favorable prices, especially if your error coins are in high demand.

Before diving into auctions, familiarize yourself with the process. Understand the fees associated with listing and selling your coins. Clearly set your minimum acceptable price to ensure a satisfactory outcome. Additionally, be prepared for the possibility of fluctuations in final prices based on bidder interest.

Private Sales: Building Personal Connections

For a more personalized approach, consider private sales. This involves directly engaging with collectors or enthusiasts who might have a keen interest in your specific error coins. Building connections within the numismatic community, either through local clubs or online forums, can lead to fruitful private sales.

In private transactions, communication is key. Clearly articulate the unique aspects of your error coins and negotiate terms that satisfy both parties. While private sales may not always fetch the highest prices, the potential for building lasting relationships with fellow collectors adds a unique dimension to the experience.

Auction Houses: Navigating High-Value Transactions

When your coins enter the realm of significant value, reaching five or six figures or more, auction houses become a compelling option. Consigning your collection to a reputable auction house opens the door to potential bidding wars among enthusiastic buyers. This competitive environment can sometimes drive prices higher than anticipated.

However, it's crucial to consider the intricacies involved. Auction houses typically charge buyer's fees and the entire process—from processing your coins to the actual auction and receiving your payment—requires patience. Before committing, it's wise to explore various auction houses, understanding their rules and requirements. Some may have a minimum consignment value, so ensure your coins meet the criteria.

DIY Online Auctions: Taking Control of Your Sales

If you prefer retail prices and want more control over the selling process without the wait associated with larger auction houses, DIY online platforms like eBay, Amazon, Esty, or MA-Shops might be your go-to solution. This option puts you in charge of photographing, listing, and shipping your coins, along with handling any customer-related issues.

While this hands-on approach demands time and effort, the advantage is that you won't need to share your profits with intermediaries, aside from potential listing or final value fees. It's a route that provides sellers with substantial control over their earnings.

In the end, your coin-collecting journey continues to evolve, and with these selling options, you can navigate the process with confidence and clarity.

How to Trade and Swap Coins

Trading and swapping coins is a delightful way to enrich your collection and engage with other passionate collectors. To kick off this enjoyable process, your first step is to connect with fellow coin enthusiasts who share an interest in trading or swapping. This can be achieved by joining local coin clubs, attending coin shows, or exploring online coin communities and forums where collectors gather.

Before diving into the trading scene, it's beneficial to have a clear vision of the coins you're seeking and those you're open to trading or swapping. Create a wish list highlighting your desired additions and a list of coins you're willing to part with to facilitate smoother negotiations.

Once you've identified potential trading partners, initiate contact and express your interest in a trade or swap. Politeness and transparency play a crucial role in these interactions. Clearly communicate the details of your collection, specifying what you have available and what you're actively searching for.

Upon finding a compatible trading partner, delve into discussions about the trade's specifics. Ensure mutual agreement on the coins involved, their conditions, and the terms of the trade, including any additional items or cash if required. Establishing clear terms upfront is key to a successful exchange.

Before sealing the deal, meticulously examine the coins involved. Confirm that they meet the pre-discussed conditions and that you are content with what you are receiving. Once both parties are satisfied, proceed to complete the trade or swap. This can be done either in person or through the mail, depending on the arrangement. If opting for mail, use secure packaging and consider insurance for added protection.

Always bear in mind that trading and swapping coins not only enhances your collection but also provides an avenue to connect with fellow collectors. This process adds diversity to your collection and elevates the enjoyment of the hobby. Success in these exchanges hinges on clear communication, trust-building, and a careful evaluation of the coins involved.

Spotting Counterfeit Coins

Entering the fascinating world of coin collecting opens the door to a realm of authenticity and history. However, amidst the genuine treasures, there lurk counterfeit coins waiting to deceive unsuspecting collectors. To safeguard your collection, here are practical ways to spot those pesky fakes.

You should start by acquainting yourself with the authentic coin's characteristics—its weight, thickness, markings, intricate designs, and diameter. If you notice any of these details seem off, exercise caution. A genuine coin has a unique identity that counterfeits struggle to replicate.

Trust your instincts. If a deal appears too good to be true, it probably is. Counterfeit coins often betray their true nature with visible casting seams, which you can sometimes spot without any magnification. If the description doesn't match the photo or the price is unbelievably low for a rare coin, consider it a red flag.

Before making a purchase, delve into the background of the company or seller. How reputable are they? How long have they been in the business? Are they associated with esteemed numismatic organizations? Answers to these questions are crucial. If something feels amiss, it's best to explore other options.

Stick to coins that have been professionally graded and authenticated by third-party graders such as PCGS or NGC. Before finalizing your purchase, verify the certification number to ensure the coin's authenticity and quality. Certified coins provide a layer of security against counterfeits.

If you're buying from online platforms like eBay, look for sellers who specialize in coins. Their expertise makes them more likely to identify fake coins. High-rated sellers who predominantly sell unrelated items may lack the necessary knowledge about coins, posing a risk to unsuspecting buyers.

Bonus Tips from the Experts

Look for the Seam: Counterfeit coins often reveal themselves through casting seams, those subtle lines that escape the notice of genuine coins. Take a close look; if you spot these seams or mysterious hole markings, it's a red flag. Authentic coins boast intricate designs consistent with their series. If something seems amiss, trust your instincts and explore other options.

Pay Close Attention to Markings: Authentic coins proudly bear mintmarks consistent with their certification. Counterfeits might fall short in this department. Before sealing the deal, dive into research about the expected marks and designs for the specific coin you're eyeing. If doubts linger, ask the seller for supporting paperwork to validate the coin's authenticity.

Find the Relief: Counterfeiters struggle to get the relief of a coin just right – it's either too high or conspicuously low. A simple test involves stacking the coin with others from the same series. If the stack wobbles, exercise caution; you might be dealing with a dubious transaction.

Opposites Attract: Nature has its ways. Magnets aren't drawn to gold and silver, so if your coin has a magnetic personality, it's probably a fraud. Keep this in mind as an extra layer of defense against counterfeits.

I'm melting!! Silver, being an excellent conductor of heat, should swiftly melt an ice cube on contact. If your "authentic" silver coin hesitates to embark on the melting process, skepticism is warranted. This simple experiment can be a revealing indicator of authenticity.

Remember, the NGC and PCGS advocate for purchasing from reputable sellers and opting for coins authenticated through their organizations. Their stamp of approval adds an extra layer of confidence to your acquisitions.

CHAPTER TEN: THE MOST LOVED AND WIDELY COLLECTED COIN SERIES
JEFFERSON NICKELS

In the world of coin collecting, Jefferson nickels hold a special allure for collectors on the lookout for valuable error coins. What might appear as an ordinary nickel at first glance could be hiding rare features that make it truly exceptional. These hidden treasures include die-breaks, missing mint marks, and the absence of key details, making each error coin a unique find.

The exciting part? You don't need a hefty budget to add these Jefferson nickels to your collection. However, it requires a mix of persistence and a touch of luck to stumble upon these elusive gems. Sometimes, during the minting process, coins aren't struck perfectly, affecting the clarity of design details. This results in certain parts of the coin's design looking a bit fuzzy, with essential details not quite clear.

Take a closer look at the reverse side of the Jefferson Nickel, and you'll find intricate details, especially on the steps of Monticello. Over time, these steps can lose definition due to wear and tear from circulation. Savvy coin collectors value nickels where the steps remain sharp and clear, often referring to them as "full steps."

To make life easier for collectors, grading services like PCGS and NGC introduced the "FS" label for Jefferson Nickels with clear steps. PCGS, for example, uses a system where a coin can receive the "FS" label if it boasts 5 or 6 clear steps. This labeling system helps collectors distinguish between coins with good strikes and those with perfect strikes. It's crucial to note that a step isn't deemed "full" if it has any blemishes like marks, or defects, or if it's unclear due to a weak strike.

The Jefferson Nickel has a fascinating history, born out of a contest initiated by the U.S. Mint in 1938. With the discontinuation of the Buffalo nickel, a coin that had circulated for twenty-five years, the Mint sought a new design to honor President Thomas Jefferson. Felix Schlag, a German immigrant, emerged as the winner, creating an iconic design that remained virtually unchanged for sixty-six years.

While the images on the coin have seen minimal alterations, the metal content underwent a temporary change during World War II. From 1942 to 1946, the war-time version of the nickel contained 56% copper, 35% silver, and 9% manganese, reflecting the scarcity of nickel due to military demands.

1938 Jefferson Nickel

Interestingly, the 1938 Jefferson Nickel wasn't the initial appearance of Thomas Jefferson on U.S. currency. His likeness had graced the two-dollar bill back in 1869. The Jefferson Nickel, with its enduring design and historical significance, remains a fascinating piece of numismatic history, encapsulating the spirit of a nation's admiration for its founding figures.

So, as you delve into the world of Jefferson nickels, keep your eyes peeled for those intriguing errors, the subtle nuances that transform an ordinary nickel into a prized possession for any collector. Each nickel tells a story, and the journey of uncovering these hidden treasures is what makes coin collecting truly captivating.

Jefferson Nickel

The Jefferson Nickel, a stalwart of American coinage, boasts distinctive features that make it a fascinating addition to any collection. Let's delve into the specifics of its composition and key dimensions:

Composition: The Jefferson Nickel is crafted from a blend of metals, with a composition comprising 75% copper and 25% nickel. This alloy not only contributes to the coin's durability but also gives it a unique appearance.

Diameter: Measuring in a diameter of 21.21 millimeters, the Jefferson Nickel occupies a compact space, making it easily distinguishable from other coins in your collection.

Thickness: At a thickness of 1.95 millimeters, the Jefferson Nickel strikes a balance between sturdiness and manageability. This thickness adds a tactile quality to the coin, enhancing the overall collecting experience.

Weight: With a weight of 5.000 grams, the Jefferson Nickel carries a substantial feel in the palm of your hand. This weight, coupled with the coin's size, contributes to its tactile appeal and makes it a delight for collectors.

Most Valuable Nickel Error Coins

If you're diving into the world of nickel collecting, it pays to know the hidden treasures that lie within certain coins. Among the vast array of nickels, some stand out for their unique errors, making them a must-have for collectors and enthusiasts. Let's explore the fascinating world of Jefferson Nickels and uncover the most valuable nickel errors.

1. 1916 Buffalo Nickel This nickel is a true gem, sought after by both collectors and miners alike. Minted in 1916, it holds a special place in the hearts of collectors due to errors on its obverse. Take a closer look, and you'll notice a double line on the Indian chief's chin and the coin's date. Minted in Philadelphia, the rarity of this coin is reflected in its price tag, reaching an impressive $431,200.

2. 1918/7-D Buffalo Nickel For those aiming to enhance their collection, the 1918/7-D Buffalo Nickel is a priority. Minted by the Denver Mint in 2018 with a 2017 die, this nickel later underwent re-striking with a proper 1918 label. The result? The number eight with a clear seven below it, making it a valuable find. With a price tag of $503,000 USD, this nickel promises substantial returns, especially in uncirculated grade.

3. 1971 No S Don't be too quick to part with the 1971 No S proof coin. This rarity from the San Francisco mint lacks the mint's S-mark, adding to its allure. Found in proof sets in 1971, this coin boasts fine finishing and luster, and its prices range from $1,000 to at least $7,637.50 USD. Consider keeping this treasure in your collection for its rarity and unique error.

4. 1939 Double Monticello Step into the world of the 1939 Double Monticello nickel, a collector's delight due to its multiple errors. On the reverse side featuring Jefferson's home, Monticello, the mint struck the word "Monticello" twice, creating a captivating overlay effect. This

Philadelphia mint creation from 1939, especially in proof version, is valued at $1,500 USD, offering collectors a unique and visually stunning addition.

5. 1945-P Doubled Die Reverse A true treasure for collectors and miners, the 1945-P Doubled Die Reverse nickel from the Philadelphia Mint boasts a double die error on the reverse. Visible in Monticello and the words "Cents" and "States of America," this gem is even more enticing in uncirculated grade. With prices ranging from $20 to at least $110 USD, this coin promises substantial profits for collectors lucky enough to own this error nickel.

6. 1943-P 3 over 2 Monticello

Let's kick off with a true gem – the 1943-P 3 over 2 Monticello. This coin is not just a piece of currency; it's a piece of history. With numerical errors on the dates, specifically a faint hit of the number 2 below the number 3 on the obverse, this coin stands out. What makes it even more remarkable is its composition – 35% silver, a rarity in 20th-century coins. Struck in 1943 at the Philadelphia Mint, its value ranges from a promising 50 USD to a noteworthy 300 USD.

7. 1955-D Jefferson Nickel

Moving on, we encounter the 1955-D Jefferson Nickel, a coin that defies the norm. The Denver mint, known for its precision, surprised collectors with the D-mark over "S" and an elegant curve. In its uncirculated state, this coin promises a profit. Struck in 1955, its value starts from a respectable 25 USD and can climb up to 45 USD.

8. 1954-S Jefferson Nickel

Our journey through error coins brings us to the 1954-S Jefferson Nickel. An intriguing error unfolds as the letter mark "S" appears over "D," with the bottom of the "D" curving out beneath the letter "S." Mint errors like these make collectors and miners value the coin more. The San Francisco mint struck this piece in 1954, and in its prime state, it commands a value of 150 USD.

9. 1949-D Jefferson Nickel

Another jewel in the over-mintmark error-coins series, the 1949-D Jefferson Nickel, boasts a captivating D-mark over "S." The "D" gracefully curves out over "S," making this 1949-D nickel error coin a scarce find in today's market. Handle it with care, and its value, ranging from 50 USD to 150 USD, will endure.

10. 1975-D High D-Mark

Our exploration concludes with the 1975-D High D-Mark, where a tiny deviation makes a significant impact. The D-mark, slightly off the mark from the Denver mint, rests on the left of the number 5. Such art errors captivate collectors and miners alike. Rare to find in uncirculated grades today, this coin, struck in 1975, commands prices starting from a modest 50 USD to a noteworthy 250 USD.

11. 1935 Buffalo Nickel

Picture this – the Philadelphia Mint striking a nickel, attempting to capture the essence of a buffalo on one side. However, the master hub doesn't cooperate entirely, resulting in a doubled impression of certain elements. The magic unfolds on the words "five cents" and the motto, drawing collectors with its distinctive charm. This 1935 Buffalo Nickel, with doubling even on the tail, has become a must-have for those completing their Buffalo Nickel series.

Key Details:

- Minted in 1935 by the Philadelphia mint.
- Uncirculated state valued at $145,900 USD.

12. 1936-D Buffalo Nickel

Moving to Denver, the 1936-D Buffalo Nickel takes center stage with a peculiar error – a buffalo with three and a half legs on the reverse. The craftsmanship of this nickel is underscored by its rarity, as the mint struck only a limited number with this unique feature. A testament to the allure of coins with unexpected quirks.

Key Details:

- Minted in 1936 by the Denver Mint.
- Valued at $22,400 USD in its best condition.

13. 1937-D Buffalo Nickel

Continuing the trend of distinctive errors, the 1937-D Buffalo Nickel takes us on a journey where polishing went a bit too far. The result? A buffalo missing a leg on the reverse. Collectors seeking coins with charming flaws find solace in this unique specimen.

Key Details:

- Minted in 1937 by the Denver Mint.
- Valued at $107,500 USD in its best state.

14. 1942-D D over Horizontal D

Behold the 1942-D Nickel, a true marvel with a re-punched mintmark error. Craftsmen initially punched the mintmark too close to Monticello, prompting a second striking. The result is a beautiful error that elevates this nickel to dream-worthy status.

Key Details:

- Gem from the Denver Mint in 1942.
- Prices range from $50 USD to $32,200 USD.

15. 1964 Jefferson Nickel

Enter the enigmatic 1964 Jefferson Nickel, an asset of unparalleled value. This coin boasts a mirror brockage error, featuring a head on both obverse and reverse, with one side resembling a mirror. The rarity of this striking error makes it a prized possession for collectors willing to invest.

Key Details:

- Minted by the Philadelphia Mint in 1964.
- Prices range from $10,000 USD to a staggering $1.15 million USD.

16. 1979-S Type I Proof

Among the rare proof coins with errors, the 1979-S Type I Proof stands out. The mushy look of the S-mark adds an element of mystery, making it a sought-after piece for collectors looking to enrich their collections.

Key Details:

- Minted by the San Francisco Mint in 1979.

- Priced between $4 USD and $375 USD.

17. 1972-D Jefferson Nickel

Closing our journey through nickel errors, the 1972-D Jefferson Nickel reveals die breaks and intriguing cuts. Mint mistakes near Jefferson's forehead add character to this rare coin, making it a wish-list item for collectors and miners alike.

Key Details:

- Minted by the Denver Mint in 1972.
- Prices start from $5.99 USD to $350 USD.

Conclusion

In the realm of coin collecting, the joy lies in completing a set enriched with nickel error coins. These gems, once in circulation, are now cherished for their rarity and unique flaws. As you navigate the world of numismatics, treasure these coins, for they hold not just historical value but also the potential for a great fortune. Remember, in the world of coin errors, every imperfection tells a story, and each coin is a chapter waiting to be explored.

WASHINGTON QUARTERS

If you've ever held a coin worth twenty-five cents, you've held a quarter. The history of the quarter is a tale that stretches back to 1796, and over the years, it has undergone various design changes. For those with an interest in the coin market, especially in the realm of quarters, luck may be on your side. Certain quarters, if you happen to own or stumble upon them, might carry more value than you'd expect. So, which quarters are worth keeping an eye out for, and why?

In the everyday hustle and bustle, one type of quarter frequently changing hands is the Washington Quarter. These quarters have been circulating since 1932, and they continued their journey in pockets and purses until 1998. Remarkably, many people still use them for everyday purchases.

While quarters are often thought of as mere pocket change, some modern ones defy this notion by holding more than their face value. These unique coins have been circulating for a significant period, adding an element of intrigue to the world of coin collecting.

The story of the Washington Quarters began in 1932 when the U.S. Mint issued the George Washington Quarter to commemorate the 200th anniversary of the first president's birth on February 22, 1732. This quarter marked a shift from its predecessor, the Standing Liberty Quarter, which was the last to feature Liberty on the obverse.

Production of the George Washington Quarter continued until 1998 when it made way for the 50 State Quarters Program in 1999. Over the years, these quarters featured different designs, with the reverse typically showcasing an eagle with wings spread wide. However, a temporary change occurred in 1975 and 1976, celebrating the bicentennial of the Declaration of Independence. During these years, the reverse displayed a colonial drummer in lieu of the customary eagle.

So, the next time you come across a Washington quarter in your pocket change, take a moment to appreciate the rich history and stories it carries. You never know; it might be more than just a quarter – it could be a piece of history worth holding onto.

Washington Quarters

If you've ever wondered about the details that make a Washington quarter what it is, here's a closer look at the composition and dimensions that define these small yet significant pieces of currency.

Composition: Washington quarters are crafted from a combination of materials, with 91.67% of the coin made of copper and the remaining 8.33% composed of nickel. This alloy blend gives the quarter its distinctive appearance and durability.

Diameter: Measuring in at 24.26 mm, the diameter of a Washington quarter is a defining feature. This specification, while seemingly small, contributes to the coin's recognizability and ease of use in daily transactions.

Thickness: With a thickness of 1.75 mm, the Washington quarter strikes a balance between being substantial enough to withstand the rigors of circulation and maintaining a slim profile that fits comfortably in pockets and coin slots.

Weight: Despite its small size, the Washington quarter weights 5.670 g. This weight, carefully calibrated, ensures that the coin feels substantial while remaining convenient for everyday use.

Most Valuable Washington Quarters Error Coins

1. 2004-D Wisconsin Quarter Extra Leaf Low Business Strike

Year: 2004

Series: State Quarters

Mint Mark: Denver

Error: Extra Leaf Low

Grade: MS 67

Date of Sale: 12th January 2020

Price: $6,000

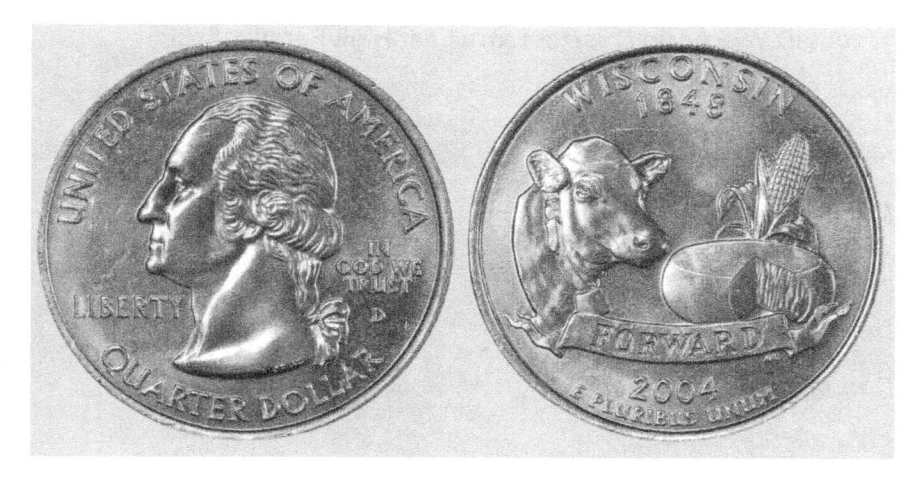

This 2004-D Wisconsin Quarter, part of the State Quarters series, holds a distinctive error – the Extra Leaf Low. Graded at MS 67, it fetched a price of $6,000 on January 12th, 2020. A fascinating piece for collectors, this quarter showcases the artistry and occasional quirks that make each coin unique.

2. 1822 Capped Bust Quarter 25/50c Regular Strike

Year: 1822

Series: Capped Bust

Mint Mark: None (Philadelphia)

Error: Denomination Struck Twice – 25c over 50c

Grade: MS 66

Date of Sale: 1st April 2009

Price: $184,000

Traveling back in time to 1822, we encounter the Capped Bust Quarter with a captivating error — Denomination Struck Twice. Graded at MS 66, this coin, sold on April 1st, 2009, for an impressive $184,000. Such errors offer a glimpse into the intricate history of coin production.

3. 2004-D Wisconsin Quarter Extra Leaf High Regular Strike

Year: 2004

Series: State Quarters

Mint Mark: Denver

Error: Extra Leaf High

Grade: MS 66

Date of Sale: 7th July 2006

Price: $2,530

Continuing our journey through the State Quarters series, the 2004-D Wisconsin Quarter with the Extra Leaf High error boasts a Grade of MS 66. Sold on July 7th, 2006, for $2,530, this coin exemplifies how subtle variations can significantly impact a coin's value.

4. 2000-P Maryland Quarter Muled With Sacagawea Dollar

Year: 2000

Series: State Quarters

Mint Mark: Philadelphia

Error: Mule – Maryland Quarter Obverse with Sacagawea Dollar Reverse

Grade: MS 67

Date of Sale: 21st March 2018

Price: $192,000

In the year 2000, a unique error emerged – the Mule with the Maryland Quarter Obverse and Sacagawea Dollar Reverse. Graded at MS 67, this coin, sold on March 21st, 2018, fetched an impressive $192,000. A fusion of different designs, this error adds a layer of intrigue to the world of coin collecting.

5. 1828 Capped Bust Quarter 25/50c Regular Strike

Year: 1828

Series: Capped Bust

Mint Mark: None (Philadelphia)

Error: Denomination Stamped Twice – 25c over 50c

Grade: MS 67+

Date of Sale: 15th November 2013

Price: $352,500

Our journey concludes with the 1828 Capped Bust Quarter, featuring a rare error – Denomination Stamped Twice. Graded at MS 67+, this coin, sold on November 15th, 2013, commanded an impressive $352,500. An embodiment of historical anomalies, this quarter invites collectors to explore the nuances of minting mishaps.

6. 1918/7-S Overdate Full Head Standing Liberty Quarter

In the coin-collecting universe, sometimes dies from different coins join forces, creating rare gems like the 1918/7-S Overdate Full Head Standing Liberty Quarter. Minted in 1918 with an overdate of 1917, this beauty from the Standing Liberty series boasts a unique error. Imagine a penny's face on a dime's reverse – that's the kind of mint mistake that turns heads. Graded at MS 64+ FH, this coin made waves in the numismatic world, selling for a whopping $336,000 on the 17th of September, 2020.

7. 2009-D District of Columbia DDR Quarter Business Strike

Not all errors are born from mismatched dies; some result from planchet-based mishaps. The 2009-D District of Columbia DDR Quarter Business Strike is a stellar example. This doubled die reverse error, striking on a blank with the wrong metal, can lead to fascinating outcomes. Picture a clad coin struck on a gold or silver planchet, and you'll grasp the allure of this mint mistake. Graded at MS 66, this coin, sold on the 10th of July, 2014, fetched a price of $3,055.

8. 1891 Seated Liberty Quarter MPD Regular Strike

The Seated Liberty series presents its treasure – the 1891 Seated Liberty Quarter MPD Regular Strike. Clad coins sometimes exhibit missing coating, creating a striking two-tone effect. Mint errors can also arise from die or planchet movements between strikes, resulting in an overstrike, off-center, or overlapping multi-strike. This 1891 beauty, with a misplaced date, achieved a grade of MS 64, selling for $1,058 on the 2nd of August, 2017.

9. 1999-P Susan B. Anthony $1 Struck On A 1999 Georgia Quarter

Dies, working tirelessly, eventually bear the marks of time – cracks and flaws called cuds. The 1999-P Susan B. Anthony $1 Struck on A 1999 Georgia Quarter showcases a unique error – a wrong planchet. Imagine a dollar coin struck on a quarter – an unexpected twist that makes this error particularly intriguing. Graded at MS 63, this coin, sold in January 2009, commanded a price of $10,925.

10. 1983-P Spitting Eagle Type 2 Clad Quarter Business Strike

Last but certainly not least, let's uncover the charm of the 1983-P Spitting Eagle Type 2 Clad Quarter Business Strike. Delving into the realm of amusing errors, this coin features a Die Clash – Spitting Eagle. A doubled eye or ear might seem funny, but it's a result of a Doubled Die Obverse (DDO), where the second strike distorts the portrait. Graded at MS 66+, this coin, auctioned on the 13th of March, 2018, fetched a price of $504.

11. 1976-D Bicentennial Quarter (1776-1976) DDO Regular Strike

Year: 1976

Series: Bicentennial Quarter

Mint Mark: Denver

Error: Doubled Die Obverse

Grade: MS 66

Date of Sale: 7th May 2023

Price: $8,400

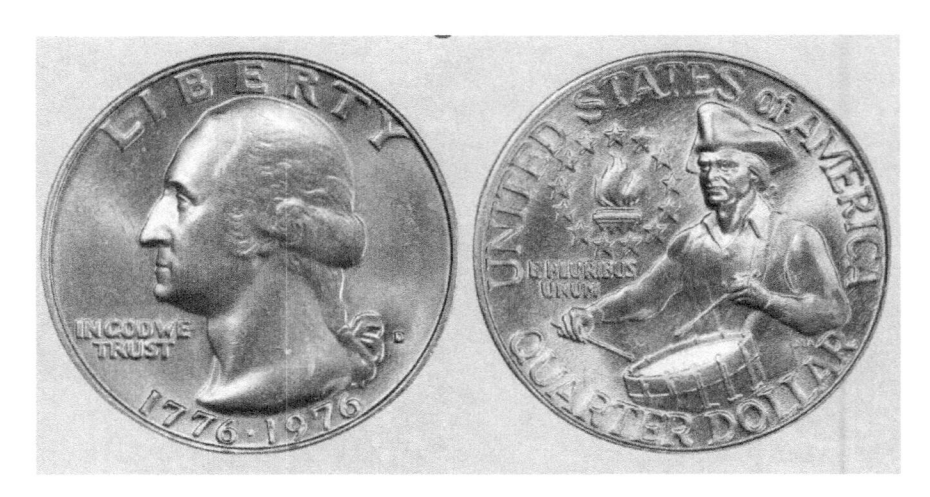

Modern coins are typically flawless, thanks to automated processes and digital design. Yet, the 1976-D Bicentennial Quarter breaks this mold with its Doubled Die Obverse. Distinguishing die doubling from planchet doubling might seem daunting, but numismatic references and experts can be your guiding light.

12. 1970-D Quarter DDO Type 2 Regular Strike

Year: 1970

Series: Washington Quarter

Mint Mark: Denver

Error: Doubled Die Obverse

Grade: MS 65

Date of Sale: 3rd January 2012

Price: $2,875

Travel back to 1970 when the US Mint marked its coins with initials, denoting their branch of origin. The 'D' for Denver carries a story of Doubled Die Obverse, making this quarter a unique piece of history.

13. 1892 S/S RPM Barber Quarter Business Strike

Year: 1892

Series: Barber Quarter

Mint Mark: San Francisco

Error: Repunched Mint Mark

Grade: MS 64

Date of Sale: 30th October 2018

Price: $1,440

Delve into the vintage charm of the 1892 S/S RPM Barber Quarter, where mint marks tell tales of repunching and overlapping. Discover the world of re-punched mint marks (RPM) and the intriguing history etched in every detail.

14. 1957-D Misplaced MM Quarter Regular Strike

Year: 1957

Series: Washington Quarter

Mint Mark: Denver

Error: Misplaced Mint Mark

Grade: MS 66+

Date of Sale: 14th July 2021

Price: $1,860

Uncover the mysteries of misplaced mint marks in the 1957-D quarter, where a slight shift during minting turns a regular strike into a captivating numismatic anomaly.

15. 1990-S Proof Deep Cameo DDO Quarter

Year: 1990

Series: Washington Quarter

Mint Mark: San Francisco

Error: Doubled Die Obverse

Grade: PR 70 DCAM

Date of Sale: 4th January 2017

Price: $7,050

Step into the realm of proof coins with the 1990-S Proof Deep Cameo DDO Quarter. The doubled die obverse adds a layer of depth to its pristine proof finish, making it a prized possession for collectors.

16. 1943 DDO Quarter Business Strike

Year: 1943

Series: Washington Quarter

Mint Mark: None (Philadelphia)

Error: Doubled Die Obverse

Grade: MS 67

Date of Sale: 22nd March 2020

Price: $22,250

Experience the rarity of the 1943 DDO Quarter, where a doubled die obverse elevates its status to an MS 67 grade, showcasing the impeccable craftsmanship of a bygone era.

17. 1942-D DDR Quarter Regular Strike

Year: 1942

Carlos Clifton

Series: Washington Quarter

Mint Mark: Denver

Error: Doubled Die Reverse

Grade: MS 66+

Date of Sale: 16th November 2012

Price: $8,225

Dive into the rich history of the 1942-D DDR Quarter, where the doubled die reverse adds a fascinating twist to this regular strike. Explore the intricacies that make each coin a unique piece of history.

LINCOLN PENNIES

In the vast landscape of American coinage, the Lincoln cent, affectionately known as the penny, stands tall as one of the most cherished and widely collected series. The journey of this iconic coin began with the introduction of the Wheat cent design, a creation that sparked a passion for coin collecting across the nation.

Crafted by the skilled hands of artist Victor David Brenner, both the front (known as the heads side) and the original back of the coin came to life under his artistic vision. Little did he know that his work would set the stage for a coin series that would capture the hearts of collectors for generations.

Collectors, both seasoned and novice, find joy in amassing these pennies, making them a cornerstone of American numismatics. Among the sought-after treasures are the famous and rare Wheat pennies, each carrying a piece of history within its metal confines.

When delving into the world of Lincoln Cents, seekers of valuable errors must keep a keen eye on specific details. The chin, eyes, and ears of these one-cent coins often hide subtle errors, cracks, cuds, or missing elements that can turn an ordinary coin into a unique find.

The Lincoln Cent series boasts thousands of die varieties, offering collectors a myriad of opportunities to discover coins that stand out from the crowd. And here's a fascinating tidbit – these coins, often considered a smart long-term investment, have the potential to appreciate significantly over time. Believe it or not, some pennies, once worth a mere cent, have transformed into valuable treasures fetching thousands of dollars.

Victor David Brenner's imprint on the U.S. Lincoln penny is unmistakable, with his famous initials "V.D.B." proudly displayed on the reverse of this beloved coin. Since its introduction into circulation in 1909, the Lincoln Cent has retained its original obverse design, marking it as the longest-running coin type in U.S. history.

However, the journey of the Lincoln Penny goes beyond its design – it's a tale woven with historical nuances and unexpected turns. Before its inception, a persistent President Theodore Roosevelt and the untimely demise of sculptor Augustus Saint-Gaudens set the stage for a new era in coinage design. The Lincoln Penny broke a longstanding American taboo by featuring the image of a real person, the revered Abraham Lincoln.

The design process, though challenging, resulted in a coin that not only honored Lincoln but also broke tradition with the inclusion of the motto "In God We Trust." The release of the Lincoln pennies in 1909 was met with anticipation and excitement, but it wasn't without its share of controversies.

The scandal over the inclusion of Brenner's initials "V.D.B." on the coin sparked public fervor, leading to a temporary halt in production and a frenzy of hoarding among collectors. The subsequent removal of these initials only added to the coin's mystique and desirability among collectors.

What adds to the thrill of collecting Lincoln pennies is the possibility of stumbling upon valuable coins in everyday pocket change. While the average coin stays in circulation for several decades, fortunate collectors have uncovered pennies from the mid-1900s during routine transactions, turning mundane moments into numismatic discoveries.

Specifications

Composition: Copper Plated Zinc 2.5% Cu Balance Zn

Weight: 2.500 g

Diameter: 0.750 in.19.05 mm

Thickness: 1.52 mm

Edge: Plain

No. of Reeds: N/A

Most Valuable Wheat Penny Error Coins

1. 1943 Wheat Penny (Bronze Cent Strike)

Imagine a time when copper was a precious resource for war, leading to the birth of an exceptional coin – the 1943 Wheat Penny with a Bronze Cent Strike. During this era, the Philadelphia Mint, in an unusual twist of fate, created pennies with bronze planchets instead of the intended zinc-coated steel. These accidental coins, a blend of copper and steel, became highly sought after by collectors.

Spotting the authenticity of a 1943 penny isn't a daunting task, and its imperfections make it a valuable piece. Be cautious, though, as counterfeit versions circulate. The highest recorded mint state price for this coin reached a staggering $1.7 million, while you can explore the market with prices ranging from $14,000 to $300,000.

2. 1909-S Over Horizontal S Wheat Penny

Travel back to the origins of the Lincoln wheat penny, specifically to the 1909-S Over Horizontal S Wheat Penny. This coin carries the distinction of being the first in its lineage to exhibit a repunch mistake. Hand-punched letters by San Francisco mint workers sometimes resulted in errors, like placing the "S" mark horizontally instead of vertically.

In a worn state, spotting this error becomes challenging, adding to its allure for collectors. Struck in San Francisco, prices for this coin start at a modest $80 and can go up to $400, depending on its mint grade.

3. 1917 Wheat Penny (Double Die)

Witness the mesmerizing double die error on the 1917 Wheat Penny's obverse. Craftsmen, working diligently at the Philadelphia mint, left a mark of their craftsmanship – a coin with doubled numbers and letters, notably in the word "TRUST." To catch this narrow double die, a 10X magnifying glass becomes your detective tool.

As a product of the Philadelphia Mint in 1917, this coin's rarity and age make it a cherished find for collectors. Prices for this intriguing piece range from $160 to $240, contingent on its condition.

4. 1944 Wheat Penny (Steel Cent Strike)

The 1944 Wheat Penny takes us back to a time of transition. Amidst the challenges of steel pennies in 1944, the US returned to the bronze alloy, but not without leaving behind a trace of zinc-plated steel planchets. This anomaly, a result of coin production overlaps with coins for Belgium, birthed a historically significant and valuable coin.

Minted in Philadelphia, San Francisco, and Denver, the 1944 penny has distinct values. The best mint state price for the 1944 Philadelphia penny is at least $50,000, while both the Denver and San Francisco mint versions command a price of at least $60,000.

5. 1955 Lincoln Wheat Penny (Double Die)

Dive into the drama of the 1955 Lincoln Wheat Penny, featuring a double die error on its obverse. The doubling affects both the date and the motto, creating a visually striking coin. Although craftsmen usually catch such errors before circulation, the 1955 version made its way into collectors' hearts.

Minted in Philadelphia, this coin is a favorite among collectors, with prices ranging from $500 to $2,600. Given its popularity, beware of deceptive versions circulating in the market.

6. 1982-D Wheat Penny (Copper Small Date)

Imagine finding a seemingly ordinary wheat penny in your pocket, only to discover it holds a rare error. The 1982-D Wheat Penny, with its top-aligned numerals and perfectly matched bottom numbers, stands out due to a unique error during minting.

Interestingly, the Denver Mint wasn't supposed to produce bronze Lincoln pennies in 1982. Yet, some leftover copper planchets found their way into production, creating this rare and valuable error. The coin's rarity is enhanced by its captivating luster, making it a favorite among numismatists.

- Year: 1982
- Mint: Denver
- Price Range: $10,000 to $30,000

7. 1983 Lincoln Wheat Penny (Double Die)

The 1983 Lincoln Wheat Penny holds a secret beneath its surface – a double die error on the reverse side. Craftsmen at the mint accidentally struck the coin twice, causing some lettering, like "ONE CENT," to overlap. This imperfection, visible with a magnifying glass, adds allure for collectors and enthusiasts alike.

These coins are hard to come by today, underscoring their high value.

- Year: 1983
- Mint: Philadelphia
- Price Range: $75 to $275

8. 1992-D Close AM Wheat Penny

Spotting the error on a 1992-D Close AM Wheat Penny isn't a walk in the park, making it a special and valuable find. Look closely at the coin's reverse, and you'll notice the A and M letters touching – a tiny detail that captivates collectors, often requiring a 10X magnifying glass.

- Year: 1992
- Mint: Denver
- Price: At least $500 in mint state

9. 1999 Wide AM Wheat Penny

In a delightful twist, the 1999 Wide AM Wheat Penny from the Philadelphia Mint boasts an opposite error. The letters A and M are wide, contrary to the normal design where they touch. This unintended flaw, a mistake in regular circulation, has become a beauty for collectors.

- Year: 1999
- Mint: Philadelphia
- Price Range: $45 to $500, depending on mint grade

10. 1972 Wheat Penny (Double Die)

The 1972 Wheat Penny from the Philadelphia Mint showcases the famous double die error on the obverse side. Widespread imperfections in letterings and the date make this coin easily noticeable, contributing to its higher market value.

- Year: 1972
- Mint: Philadelphia
- Best Price: $14,400

11. 2000 Wide AM Wheat Penny

The year 2000 brought forth a wheat penny with a distinctive wide AM gap error between the letters on the reverse side. Notably, the letters FG are positioned closer to the Lincoln memorial structure at the bottom left. While these details are typically found on special proof coins, this error slipped into some of the circulating ones. Struck by the Philadelphia Mint, these pennies can be acquired, with prices starting from a modest $23.

12. 1998 Wide AM Wheat Penny

In 1998, the Philadelphia Mint contributed to the wheat penny saga with the wide AM error on the obverse side. The letters in the word "AMERICAN" are notably broader, a result of using a special proof die for regular coin striking. Although this error is not rare, its market value remains on the lower side, with prices starting as low as $15.

13. 1984 Lincoln Wheat Penny (Double Ear)

Step back to 1984, where a unique error captured the attention of collectors – the double ear on the Lincoln wheat penny. With a double-die fault around the second earlobe, this coin boasts high demand and a commensurate price tag. For a coin in good mint grade, expect to buy or sell it for at least $230, crafted by the Philadelphia Mint.

14. 1995 Lincoln Wheat Penny (Double Die)

In 1995, another wheat penny joined the ranks of intriguing errors. This time, the doubling flaw is visible on the layered lettering of "Liberty" on the obverse side. To appreciate this error fully, a magnifying glass might come in handy. Philadelphia Mint produced a limited number of these coins with doubling flaws, and they are relatively accessible, priced between $45 and $50.

15. 1961-D Lincoln Wheat Penny (D Over Horizontal D)

Wheat pennies with rare errors are a collector's delight, and the 1961-D penny from the Denver Mint is no exception. Featuring a secondary D-mark more visibly through the over-horizontal-D variation, this coin's strong repunch makes it a coveted addition to any collection. Prices range from $10 to $60, depending on the mint state.

16. 1922-D Lincoln Wheat Penny (No Mint Mark)

Travel back to 1922, where a wheat penny from the Denver Mint stands out for its lack of a mint mark. In the aftermath of a fire at the Philadelphia Mint, this unique error emerged. With prices ranging from $350 to a staggering $17,300, this coin's rarity and market value make it a prized possession for collectors.

In conclusion, Lincoln wheat pennies are not just pieces of currency; they are artifacts with unique errors that add to their allure. As you explore these valuable coins, remember to tread carefully, as the market may harbor fake versions. Whether you possess the coveted 1943 bronze strike error or any other wheat penny variation, cherish them, for each coin holds its own distinct value in the world of collectors and enthusiasts.

ROOSEVELT DIMES

Dimes have been a constant in the pocket change of Americans for centuries, and among them, the Roosevelt dimes stand as a testament to history and value. The United States Mint has been minting these small yet significant coins for a considerable period, with no signs of stopping.

If you're a collector with an eye for treasure, you might find yourself drawn to Roosevelt dimes minted between 1946 and 1964. Why? These dimes, crafted from silver, hold a special allure for collectors. However, don't overlook the later versions clad in copper and nickel – they, too, carry surprising value? In fact, you might stumble upon a Roosevelt dime in your everyday change that could be worth a substantial $1,110 or even more.

The story of the "Roosevelt" theme begins in 1946, a tribute to President Franklin D. Roosevelt who had recently passed away. Released on January 30th of that year to coincide with Roosevelt's birthday, these dimes bear his profile on the obverse, while the reverse features symbols of liberty, peace, and strength in the form of a torch, olive branch, and oak branch.

Why choose the dime to honor Roosevelt? The answer lies in his advocacy for the March of Dimes, a fundraising program dedicated to polio research. Roosevelt himself battled polio, contracting the disease at the age of 39.

The journey of the dime started in 1796 with small silver coins depicting Liberty on the obverse and an eagle on the reverse. A wreath replaced the eagle in 1837, and various representations of Liberty graced the dime until the introduction of the Roosevelt design.

Noteworthy in dime history is the "Mercury" dime designed by Adolph A. Weinman, in circulation from 1916 to 1945. Liberty, donning a winged cap symbolizing freedom of thought, adorned the obverse, earning the coin its nickname due to its resemblance to the Roman god Mercury. The reverse showcased a fasces and an olive branch, representing military readiness and the pursuit of peace. The Mercury dime is celebrated as one of the most aesthetically pleasing coins in U.S. history.

In 1965, a pivotal change occurred as silver was removed from the composition of the dime, marking the era of copper-nickel clad dimes.

As you explore the world of Roosevelt dimes, it's essential to note that not all are created equal in value. Some, like proof coins without mint marks, possess the potential to elevate your collection's worth significantly. Keep an eye out for those with rim clip flaws – they, too, may surpass their face value. The journey through Roosevelt dimes is not just a stroll through history but a quest for hidden treasures that might just be hiding in your pocket change.

Specifications

Composition: Cupro-Nickel 8.33% Ni Balance Cu

Weight: 2.268 g

Diameter: 0.705 in. 17.91 mm

Thickness: 1.35 mm

Edge: Reeded

No. of Reeds: 118

Most Valuable Dime Error Coins

1. 1942/1 Mercury Dime (Overdate)

Imagine holding a piece of history where the year itself becomes a captivating puzzle. The 1942/1 Mercury Dime boasts a striking overdate error that enchants collectors. Minted in Philadelphia, the workers inadvertently punched a number 1 and later added a number 2, creating a mesmerizing overlap. In the world of coin auctions, this over-the-date error stands out, attracting enthusiasts. Prices for this historical gem range from 400 USD to 2500 USD, depending on its condition.

2. 1968-S Roosevelt Dime (No Mintmark)

Step into the realm of the 1968-S Roosevelt Dime, a coin with a mystery – it bears no mintmark. Crafted in limited numbers at the San Francisco mint, these dimes are a rare find in today's coinage market. Beyond their error and rarity, the sheer beauty of these dimes, especially in their best mint state, is awe-inspiring. Holding one of these coins may mean holding a fortune, with prices soaring up to 31,300 USD.

3. 1975-S Roosevelt Dime (No Mintmark)

Continuing the saga of dimes with missing mintmarks, the 1975-S Roosevelt Dime from San Francisco is a treasure for collectors seeking to complete their list of mintmark-less dimes. Rarity defines this coin in today's market, promising a valuable return if kept in excellent condition. Prices for this dime range from 4 USD to a significant 4000 USD, making it a prized possession for lucky collectors.

4. 1982 Roosevelt Dime (No Mintmark)

In the early '80s, the Philadelphia Mint introduced the "P" mark on its coins. However, the 1982 Roosevelt Dime breaks the mold, lacking the mintmark. Struck in 1982, these error coins, shipped to Ohio, are a testament to the scarcity of such coins in circulation. Collectors are drawn to these historical anomalies, valuing them for their unique place in the timeline. Prices for circulated versions start at 55 USD, while uncirculated ones command at least 175 USD.

5. 1988-D Dime (Repunch Mintmark)

Witness the allure of repunched coins with the 1988-D Dime from the Denver Mint. Craftsmen left impressions that overlap, creating a visually stunning mistake that collectors cherish. Rare and in demand, this gem from 1988 commands a hefty price, reaching at least 800 USD in the best mint state. With only a few of these coins surviving today, owning one could mean a substantial profit in the world of coinage and collectibles.

6. 1983-S Roosevelt Dime (No Mintmark)

Delve into the beauty of proof coins with the 1983-S Roosevelt Dime, where the absence of the mintmark adds to its allure. Minted in San Francisco, these proof coins, not intended for circulation, have become rare collectibles with a deep frosted touch. Beyond their scarcity, the exquisite design makes these dimes valuable, with prices ranging between 10,000 USD and an impressive 20,490 USD.

7. 1964-D Roosevelt Proof Dime (No Mintmark)

First up, we have the 1964-D Roosevelt Proof Dime without the telltale "D" mintmark. It's a bit like finding a hidden treasure – the Denver Mint accidentally skipped the mark on some of these proof coins. Although it's a common error, collectors always have a soft spot for these unique dimes.

Since they're proof coins, they're not your everyday pocket change. Expect rarity and high value, with prices ranging from a cool $525 to $6495. These silver gems were crafted by the Denver mint back in 1964.

8. 1967 Roosevelt Dime (Double Die and Rim Clip)

Next on our list is the 1967 Roosevelt Dime with not one, but two errors — a double die and a rim clip. Imagine finding a coin with a little extra character! Despite these quirks, PCGS grades this coin at a high mint state level. The doubling shows up on the "IN GOD WE TRUST" lettering and "JS" under Roosevelt's neck, making it a must-have for collectors.

The rim clip? That's a result of a hiccup in the minting process. This error-packed dime can be yours for at least $69 if you snag the clipped version. But if you want the one with the doubling error, be prepared to shell out at least $600. Crafted by the Philadelphia Mint in 1967, these dimes are truly one-of-a-kind.

9. 1969-D Roosevelt Dime (Double Struck)

Now, let's talk about the 1969-D Roosevelt Dime with a fascinating error – it's double-struck! The mint messed up the first time, placing the details on the wrong planchet. The result? A coin with details 90% off-center after the second strike. It's not just that; these coins also come with a straight clip on the sides, adding to their unique charm.

For collectors and miners alike, this error coin is a gem. Expect a hefty price tag of at least $100 for this rare find from the Denver Mint in 1969.

10. 1969-D/D Roosevelt Dime (Repunched)

Moving on to the 1969-D/D Roosevelt Dime – a collector's dream! Why? Because of a rare repunching error on the top right part of the "D." Mistakes like these usually keep coins out of circulation, but this lucky dime from the Denver Mint slipped through, making it a low-numbered rarity.

If you're fortunate enough to own one, cherish it – and if you ever decide to part with it, you're in for a good payday. Minted in 1969, this repunched dime fetches at least $100 in the best mint state.

11. 1970-S Roosevelt Dime (No Mintmark)

Also, we have the 1970-S Roosevelt Dime without its mintmark "S." Mint mistakes are rare, but when they happen, they turn coins into coveted collectibles. The San Francisco Mint accidentally left out the mark on this proof dime, and only 2000 pieces were made as collectibles, not for everyday use.

12. 1969-D Roosevelt Dime (Missing Clad Layer)

Ever heard of a dime missing its clad layers? The 1969-D Roosevelt Dime is one such rarity. Some of these dimes, minted in Denver, boast missing clad layers either on the reverse or obverse. It's an error that catches the eye and promises a delightful profit. The rarity factor adds to the allure, making these dimes sought after by collectors. Prices dance between 50 USD to a minimum of 62 USD, depending on their mint state.

13. 1965 Roosevelt Dime (Transitional Error)

In the midst of transitioning from silver to clad metal in 1965, a peculiar error emerged. The 1965 Roosevelt Dime, usually clad, decided to defy the norm and don a silver body. With no mintmark, collectors speculate that the Philadelphia Mint is behind this unique creation. An imperfection turned this dime into a one-of-a-kind treasure. The US mint birthed them in 1965, and today, a dime in the best mint state commands a staggering 8625 USD.

14. 1998 Bonded Group of Roosevelt Dimes

A bonding mishap at the mint resulted in a fascinating ensemble – the 1998 Bonded Group of Roosevelt Dimes. Thirty-two dimes, originally intended as separate entities, were bonded together during the minting process. A quirky error that excites collectors and miners alike. Struck in Philadelphia in 1998, this rare error gem demands a higher price due to its uniqueness, with a notable best price tag of 9200 USD.

15. 1999-D Roosevelt Dime (Wrong Strike)

Prepare to be intrigued by the 1999-D Roosevelt Dime, a coin that defies expectations with its captivating errors. Instead of the expected silver hue, this dime boasts a distinctive brown color, a result of a too-large planchet. Minted in San Francisco in 1999, this captivating error coin is a collector's delight, commanding a favorite price of 14375 USD.

Carlos Clifton

16. 1942/1-D Mercury Dime (Overdate)

Witness history in the form of the 1942/1-D Mercury Dime – an overdate marvel created by the Denver Mint. The accidental placement of the number 2 over number 1 adds a layer of intrigue to this treasure. The rarity of such errors makes this coin highly sought after, fetching prices ranging from 400 USD to a staggering 6,900 USD.

STATE QUARTERS

Imagine taking a cross-country coin-collecting road trip that lasts a decade. Well, that's precisely what the 50 State Quarters Program offered to enthusiasts and collectors alike. Launched in 1999 as a 10-year initiative, this program was a unique celebration of the diverse heritage of each of the 50 states in the United States.

The United States Mint played a key role in this adventure by issuing five new quarters annually. The order of issuance followed the sequence in which states ratified the Constitution or joined the Union. So, every year brought a fresh set of quarters, each unveiling the rich history and identity of a different state.

Now, let's flip the coin to explore the design. On the reverse side of each quarter, you'll find a unique illustration representing the chosen state. It's like a tiny canvas showcasing the essence of that particular corner of the country. However, don't expect to find George Washington hanging out on the reverse side – he's holding down the fort on the obverse since 1932.

Speaking of the obverse, in a nifty move to make room for the state designs, the usual inscriptions – "UNITED STATES OF AMERICA," "QUARTER DOLLAR," "LIBERTY," and "IN GOD WE TRUST" – relocated to the obverse side. It's a coin-collecting journey where even the layout gets a creative twist!

The excitement didn't stop with the original 50 states. In 2009, the Mint extended the adventure with an extra set of quarters. This time, they paid tribute to Washington, DC, and the five U.S. territories. It was like a bonus chapter in the coin-collecting novel, adding a special touch to the District of Columbia and U.S. Territories Quarters Program.

So, if you ever come across these quarters in your collection, know that you're holding onto a piece of America's vibrant history. Each quarter is more than just currency – it's a tiny, yet powerful, gateway to the heart and soul of a state or territory.

Most Valuable State Quarters Error Coins

Coin collecting isn't just about filling albums with shiny discs; it's about discovering the hidden treasures that make each coin unique. The State Quarters series, a highlight in the coin collecting world, has its own share of rare gems. In this chapter, we explore some of the most valuable State Quarters that have captured the attention of collectors and enthusiasts alike.

1. 2005-P Minnesota Quarter (Double Die Error)

The 2005-P Minnesota Quarter, with its double die error, has become a coveted gem among collectors. The mistake adds a touch of beauty to the coin, making it more than just an error – it's a work of art. Some of these coins feature an extra treetop next to the fourth evergreen, a result of the double die during the minting process in Philadelphia in 2005. The doubling effect has made this coin highly sought after, with values ranging from 100 to 800 USD.

2. 1999-P Delaware Quarter (Spitting Horse)

The 1999-P Delaware Quarter boasts a unique error known as the "Spitting Horse." A raised line extends from the horse's mouth, creating an eye-catching mistake between the letters A and E in "CAESAR." Minted in Denver in 1999, these quarters, though common, hold significant value, especially when in pristine mint state. Prices in the market start from 10 USD and can go up to 500 USD.

3. 1999-P Connecticut Quarter (Rare and Wrong Strike)

The 1999-P Connecticut Quarter distinguishes itself with a rare and wrong strike. The error, located at the end of the feeder's finger, adds a layer of intrigue to this seemingly ordinary coin. Minted in Philadelphia for Connecticut State in 1999, the best price for this quarter reached a remarkable 3720 USD in 2020.

4. 1999-P New Jersey Quarter (Wrong Strike)

Among the Philadelphia Mint's creations is the 1999-P New Jersey Quarter, struck on a wrong planchet. This rarity, minted on a planchet meant for another country, attracts collectors willing to pay substantial sums for this special piece. With a best price of 13,200 USD, these quarters are hard to find due to the limited number struck in 1999.

5. 1999-P Susan B. Anthony Dollar (Wrong Strike)

The 1999-P Susan B. Anthony Dollar is a high-priced rarity, thanks to a unique coinage error. Minted in Philadelphia, the coin's details were intended for a blank planchet but ended up on a Georgia quarter, creating an intriguing piece of history. In the best mint state, this coin can fetch an impressive 6325 USD.

6. 2000-P Maryland Quarter (Wrong Strike)

The 2000-P Maryland Quarter showcases the result of striking details on a smaller-sized planchet, creating an unusual and visually striking coin. Minted in Philadelphia in 2000, the coin's imperfections, including an off-center George Washington's head, contribute to its high market value, reaching 6325 USD in the best mint state.

7. 2000-P Sacagawea Dollar (Striking Error)

Dreaming of owning a US mule quarter coin? Look no further. The 2000-P Sacagawea Dollar is a collector's dream, being the first mule coin ever released by the US. What makes it special? A striking error – the mint used dies not intended for this coin, making it a rare find. This rarity translates to a high value, with the best price hitting a whopping $192,000 in 2018. A true gem from the Philadelphia Mint.

8. 2007-P Wyoming Quarter (Double Die Error)

The 2007-P Wyoming Quarter is a subtle beauty with errors not easily visible to the naked eye. Take a closer look with a magnifying glass, and you'll discover various doublings around the saddle horn image on the reverse. The artistic allure of this coin makes it a sought-after item for collectors. Minted by Philadelphia in 2007, this coin, in its best mint state, can fetch around $422.99.

9. 2002-P Indiana Quarter (Strike on the Planchet)

Spotting the error on the 2002-P Indiana Quarter is a breeze for any coin enthusiast. Instead of the correct planchet, the Philadelphia Mint struck it on a dime, resulting in an incomplete image with missing edges. Despite the mint mishap, this coin is now a perfect collectible, highly valued due to its rarity. Minted for Indiana in 2002, its price for the best mint state can soar to $4025.

10. 2004-D Wisconsin Quarter (Extra Leaf)

The 2004-D Wisconsin Quarter is a captivating piece with a double die error, showcasing a cow, a corn ear, and a block of cut cheese. The unique error? An extra cornstalk leaf above the cheese, caused by an accidental addition of more metal shavings during striking. A delightful mistake that adds character. Minted by Denver in 2004, this coin can fetch up to $6000 for the low leaf error and $2530 for the high leaf.

11. 2005 Kansas Quarter Error

The 2005 Kansas Quarter stands out with an uncommon error – missing letters from "IN GOD WE TRUST," turning it into a whimsical "IN GOD WE RUST." Collectors appreciate this beautiful error, possibly caused by grease on the machines during striking. A 2005 gem from the Philadelphia Mint, prices for this unique coin range from $2 to at least $50.

12. 2006 Colorado Quarter (Cud Error)

Finally, the 2006 Colorado Quarter boasts a cud error, a bump from an unintended die, making it a rare find for collectors. Keep an eye on the coin's reverse quarter, particularly at the three o'clock position on the inner side of the rim. Minted by Philadelphia in 2006, prices for this intriguing coin range from $5 to $35, depending on cud size and condition.

13. 2006-P North Dakota Quarter (Steel Washer Strike)

Picture this: a quarter with a hole in the middle. That's the uniqueness of the 2006-P North Dakota Quarter. Hailing from the Philadelphia Mint, this coin is a true rarity. The workers, instead of striking the details on the quarter's planchet, accidentally did it on a steel washer. Whether it was a fluke or intentional, the mystery adds to its allure.

Few of these coins made it into circulation, making them a rare find today. The demand among collectors is high, and so is the price. In its best mint state, you're looking at a coin valued at $8625 USD. A true gem from 2006.

14. 2006-P Nevada Quarter (Striking Error)

The 2006-P Nevada Quarter not only boasts one of the best statehood designs but also carries a unique striking error. The irregular and non-circular shapes on the planchet quarter are a result of straight or curved coin blanks. The error occurred during the cutting process, creating straight-clipped planchets.

Collectors rejoice in owning this distinct coin with its planchet irregularities, which only add to its value. Struck by the Philadelphia Mint in 2006, the coin's crisp state can fetch a starting price of at least $395 USD.

15. 2008 Arizona Quarter (Die Break)

For collectors with an eye for die-break error coins, the 2008 Arizona Quarter is a must-have. This coin features an extra cactus leaf on the reverse, along with cud errors covering parts of the date. More die breaks and larger cuds equate to a higher coin value.

Struck by the Philadelphia Mint for Arizona in 2008, these unique errors make the coin more valuable. Prices for this intriguing piece range from $10 USD to $150 USD.

16. 2009-D District of Columbia Quarter (Double Die Error)

Carlos Clifton

Denver Mint error coins often capture collectors' hearts, and the 2009-D District of Columbia Quarter is no exception. As part of the Washington DC and US quarters program, this coin stands out with a strong doubling of "ELL" in Ellington's name and vivid doubling on the piano keys.

Made of silver and released in a mint state, this coin commands a high value. For those fortunate enough to possess the 2009-D District of Columbia Quarter, prices start at $75 USD, reaching up to an impressive $4000 USD for the best specimens. A valuable addition to any collection from 2009.

Carlos Clifton

CHAPTER ELEVEN: ADVANCED TIPS FOR PROFITABLE COIN COLLECTING
Investing in Rare Coins

Rare Coins That Are Worth Money

Imagine stumbling upon an old piggy bank in your attic, and voila! Rare coins worth millions. Well, while that might be more of a numismatic fantasy, it's not entirely impossible. The United States Mint has been crafting coins since 1794, and you never know what hidden gems might be waiting to be discovered.

The journey of American coinage is fascinating. Gold and silver were the primary metals until the 20th century, shaping the bimetallic standard. Gold faced a ban in coinage after Executive Order 6102 in 1933, while silver lingered on as commodity money in the U.S. until the early 1970s. This rich history opens the door to the possibility of finding coins with value, tucked away in forgotten places like old drawers or your grandparent's safe deposit box.

The link between rarity and value is as straightforward as supply and demand. Numismatists worldwide seek rare specimens that tell stories of bygone eras. The more unique and historically rich a coin is, the more valuable it becomes. Whether it's one of the earliest silver coins from the U.S. Mint or a coin with a royal past, rarity, and demand create a perfect storm for high prices.

For instance, consider a regular strike 1799 Draped Bust Silver Dollar with a mintage of 423,515 and approximately 8,000 surviving specimens. On the flip side, an 1840 Liberty Head Quarter Eagle had a mintage of only 18,859 and a survival rate of only 80 across all grades. Despite being rarer, the 1840 Quarter Eagle didn't fetch as high a price as the more common 1799 Silver Dollar, proving that demand plays a crucial role.

Now, let's delve into some rarities. These are not just valuable; they are the unicorns of the coin world, often reaching the seventh or even eighth digit's worth.

1792 Silver Center Cent J-1 (Special Strike)

- Mintage: Unknown
- Survival Estimate: 25
- Face Value: 1 cent
- Composition: Copper with a silver center
- Record Sale: $2,520,000

This pattern coin from 1792, with an experimental silver center, is a testament to the Mint's testing phase before regular cent minting in 1793.

1795 Eagle BD-4 13 Leaves $10 (Regular Strike)

- Mintage: Unknown
- Survival Estimate: 20
- Face Value: $10

- Composition: 91.7% Gold, 8.3% Copper
- Record Sale: $2,585,000

A variation of the Eagle Coin from the first year of the $10 denomination minting in 1795, this rare beauty fetched an astounding $2,585,000 in a 2015 auction.

These are just snippets of the rarities awaiting discovery. So, who knows? Your pocket change might be harboring one of these hidden treasures.

1907 Extremely High Relief Double Eagle $20 (Proof)

Mintage: 16 to 22

estimate: 15

Face Value: $20

Composition: 90%Gold, 10%Copper

Record sale: $3,600,000

Behold the majesty of the 1907 Extremely High Relief Double Eagle! Crafted by the skilled hands of Augustus Saint-Gaudens, this $20 beauty is a numismatic masterpiece. Only a handful were proofed in February 1907 to test the dies, with one unique specimen featuring a plain edge, making it a true collector's dream.

1913 Liberty Head Nickel (Proof)

Mintage: 5Survival estimate: 5

Face Value: 5 cents

Composition: 75% Copper, 25% Nickel

Record sale: $4,560,000

Step into the mystery of the 1913 Liberty Head Nickel, a coin that defied its era. With the official shift to the Buffalo Nickel in 1913, no Liberty Heads were meant to be minted. Yet, five mysteriously appeared in 1920, sparking debates about their origin. Were they pattern coins or unauthorized creations by mint officials? One even made a cameo in the iconic TV series Hawaii Five-O.

1804 Class I Draped Bust Silver Dollar $1 (Proof)

Mintage: 8

Survival estimate: 8

Face Value: $1

Composition: 90% Silver, 10% Copper

Record sale: $7,680,000

Travel back to 1804 with the Class I Draped Bust Silver Dollar, a coin with a diplomatic tale. Crafted in the 1930s for diplomatic gifts to Eastern Asia, these dollars became a numismatic sensation. Some unauthorized replicas surfaced, but the original 8, identified by proper edge lettering, hold the true allure.

1944-S Steel Lincoln Penny 1C (Regular Strike)

Mintage: Unknown

Survival estimate: 2

Face Value: 1 cent

Composition: Zinc-coated Steel

Witness the wartime rarity of the 1944-S Steel Lincoln Penny. With copper reserved for war essentials in 1943, steel pennies emerged. In 1944, some steel blanks found their way into the presses, creating an exceptionally rare coin. Only two specimens with the San Francisco mint mark have stood the test of time.

These coins aren't just pocket change; they're elusive treasures with stories to tell. So, keep your eyes peeled – you never know when you might come across a piece of history that's worth a small fortune!

1943-D Bronze Lincoln Wheat Cent 1C (Regular Strike)

Let's start with a coin that defies the norm – the 1943-D Bronze Lincoln Wheat Cent. This penny, with an unexpected composition of 95% Copper and 5% Tin and Zinc, is a rare gem. Struck with leftover bronze blanks from 1942, only one specimen from the Denver Mint is known. Imagine, its record sales reached an impressive $840,000! A quirky twist of fate by a mint employee makes this coin a true collector's dream.

1787 Brasher Doubloon $15, Breast Punch (Regular Strike)

Moving on to a coin with a touch of history – the 1787 Brasher Doubloon. Crafted by jeweler Ephraim Brasher in New York, these coins were created to showcase designs proposed for the State's coinage. With a face value of $15 and a composition of 89% gold, 6% silver, 3% copper, and trace elements, these doubloons are rare finds. One with the "EB" punch on the breast sold for a staggering $2,990,000, making it a historic and valuable piece.

1838 Seated Liberty Quarter 25C, No Drapery (Proof)

Now, let's explore a quarter that stands out – the 1838 Seated Liberty Quarter, a proof version with no drapery on Lady Liberty's left arm. With a meager mintage of 3, only one of these proof coins has survived. Its uniqueness and scarcity make it a prized possession, with a record sale of $381,875.

1885 Trade Dollar T$1 (Proof)

Venturing into international trade, we encounter the 1885 Trade Dollar. Minted in limited quantities (5 to be exact), these coins were intended for overseas transactions. With a face value of $1 and composed of 90% Silver and 10% Copper, these proof versions have fetched incredible amounts, with a record sale of $3,960,000.

9. 1804 Eagle $10 Plain 4, Deep Cameo (Proof)

Step back in time to the 1804 Eagle, a $10 gold coin with a deep cameo effect. Mintage is incredibly low, with only 6 known to exist. Minted possibly in the 1830s as diplomatic gifts, one specimen with deep cameo effects sold for a staggering $5,280,000 in January 2021.

1861 Double Eagle $20 Paquet Reverse (Regular Strike)

Finally, meet the 1861 Double Eagle with a Paquet Reverse. Engraver Anthony Paquet proposed changes that never made it into circulation. Only two surviving specimens exist from the Philadelphia Mint, making them exceptionally rare. With a face value of $20, these coins achieved a remarkable record sale of $7,200,000.

CHAPTER TWELVE: COMMON PITFALLS AND HOW TO AVOID THEM

Embarking on a coin collecting journey is a thrilling endeavor filled with the promise of discovery and enjoyment. However, like any pursuit, it comes with its share of pitfalls, especially for beginners. In this chapter, we'll shed light on the top 5 common mistakes that coin collectors often make and, more importantly, guide you on how to steer clear of them.

While collecting coins can be immensely enjoyable, there's a delicate balance between the joy of the hobby and the inadvertent missteps that can affect the value of your collection. Whether you're just starting or have been immersed in numismatics for a while, understanding and avoiding these pitfalls is crucial.

In the world of coin collecting, information, tips, and tricks abound. But with great potential for enjoyment comes the responsibility to safeguard your collection from potential damage. Join us as we explore some of the biggest threats to your coins and unveil strategies to ensure the safety and value of your cherished collection.

It's a universal truth in both hobbies and professions that there's room for improvement, regardless of your expertise level. Coin collecting is no exception. Whether you're a novice or an experienced collector, the opportunity to refine your skills and expand your knowledge is ever-present. In the dynamic realm of numismatics, continuous improvement makes the journey exciting and the hobby all the more rewarding.

Overcoming Beginner Mistakes

Coin collecting is a fascinating journey, but like any adventure, it comes with its own set of challenges. In this chapter, we'll explore the 12 most common mistakes beginners make in coin collecting and provide practical solutions to help you avoid these pitfalls.

Collecting Without a Solid Understanding of Coins

Many enthusiasts dive into the world of coin collecting without a strong foundation of knowledge. It's tempting to skip the learning phase and jump straight into the excitement of buying and selling. However, this shortcut can lead to decisions influenced by assumptions and misinformation.

Solution: Do Your Homework

Take the time to educate yourself about numismatics. Unpack confusing jargon, familiarize yourself with coin-related concepts and understand industry terminology. Whether through books, guides, or interactive methods like webcasts, tailor your learning approach to your style.

Not Adhering to Proper Coin Care Protocol

Proper coin care is essential for maintaining the longevity and collectibility of your treasures. Incorrect handling or storage can inadvertently damage a coin's surface, affecting its grade on the Sheldon Scale.

Solution: Learn Which Practices Are Detrimental

Research and analyze your collectible coins before cleaning them. Use lint-free cotton gloves to handle coins, as oils from human hands can harm them. Consider your living situation, insurance options, and budget when deciding on storage methods.

Mistaking Unrealistic Expectations for Realistic Expectations

Managing expectations is crucial in coin collecting. Unrealistic goals related to the speed of growing your collection can lead to financial challenges or an unsatisfying collection.

Solution: Remain True to Your "Why" and "What"

Define your purpose behind collecting—whether it's a hobby, investment, or a mix of both. Understand your budget, timeline, and interests to create realistic expectations. Consider what holds value for you personally, whether it's monetary or sentimental.

Deprioritizing Your Interests In Favor of the Opinions of Others

While the numismatic community is supportive, it's essential to stay true to your interests. Being swayed by others' opinions can result in inauthentic decisions for your collection.

Solution: Use Your Interests as Your North Star

Your interests make your collection unique. Whether it's traditional or unconventional coins, follow what genuinely piques your interest. Avoid getting caught up in others' preferences and opinions.

Losing Focus

Coin collecting requires planning and strategy. Without focus, it's challenging to get the most out of your passion and stay within your budget.

Solution: Know What You Already Own and What You Want

Stay organized by documenting your current collection. Avoid duplicates and pieces that don't fit your theme. Create a wishlist for future acquisitions, and monitor various sources for new additions to your collection. Planning and organization will keep your collecting journey on track.

Mishandling Your Coins

Have you ever been warned not to touch your coins too much? It's not just an old collector's tale. Mishandling coins, especially raw ones, can lead to damage and wear. The incorrect way? Pinching the coin with your bare hands. Instead, use a better alternative—pinch the diameter by placing your thumb and pointer finger on the edge. For the utmost care, wear thin cotton gloves while handling coins. This not only protects them from skin oils but also prevents scratches.

Cleaning Your Coins

The condition of a coin is crucial, but attempting to clean it can do more harm than good. From acids to cleaning cloths, various methods have been tried, often with significant risks. The solution? Simple—avoid cleaning your coins. If you have a rare coin that needs cleaning, trust professionals like the Numismatic Conservation Service (NCS) to handle it with care.

Improper Storage Conditions

Where and how you store your coin collection matters. Moisture and extreme temperatures, like those in basements and attics, can damage coins. Opt for a dry place with a consistent, moderate temperature. Avoid sunlight, as it can affect a coin's condition. Ideal storage locations include a personal safe on a main level or a safety deposit box at the bank. Use quality containers like slabs or coin capsules, avoiding 2x2 holders that may react with copper coins.

Selling Too Quickly

Patience is key when it comes to selling your coins. Rushing into a sale, especially at a pawn shop or a "cash for gold" setup, may result in a lower value for your collection. Wait for the right opportunity to sell to another collector or a reputable coin dealer. This approach often yields better returns on your investment.

Following Baseless Tips

Imagine investing your life's savings in stocks because a friend said it's a surefire way to make millions. Well, coin collecting operates under a similar principle. Unless the advice comes from a seasoned numismatist or a certification service expert, be cautious. Avoid baseless information that could lead to losses instead of gains. Predicting which coins will be in demand tomorrow, let alone in a decade, is a tricky business. Trust credible sources for guidance.

Making Dead-End Investments

The allure of "low mintage" claims often lures collectors. However, low mintage doesn't guarantee rarity. Before acquiring a coin with impressive details, like an 18-karat gold piece featuring a majestic dove, ask a crucial question: will others want this coin? Your collection might be passed on or sold eventually. If there's no demand for that seemingly rare coin, your investment might be in vain. Consider the long-term appeal of each piece.

Negligence and Naivety

Cleaning old coins is a delicate art. Stories abound of enthusiasts inadvertently ruining precious coins by using harsh or abrasive solutions. Trying to restore a coin's original luster might have the opposite effect. Silver coins, in particular, lose their sheen when polished. Organizations like NGC and PCGS frown upon such actions, as the patina on an old coin contributes to its allure. Don't let negligence and naivety diminish the value of your collectibles. Treat them with care and respect their history.

CONCLUSION
Celebrating Your Successes

As we come to the end of this beginner's guide to collecting rare coins and discovering valuable errors in pocket change, it's time to celebrate your successes as a budding numismatist. Building a coin collection from scratch is no small feat, and the journey you've undertaken is a testament to your passion for the art and history encapsulated in these small, valuable treasures.

Take a moment to reflect on the coins you've acquired, the knowledge you've gained, and the joy that comes with uncovering hidden gems in your pocket change. Whether you've found rare coins, valuable errors, or simply expanded your collection with unique pieces, each acquisition is a milestone in your numismatic journey.

Part of the beauty of coin collecting is the community that surrounds it. Consider reaching out to fellow collectors, whether locally or online, to share your successes and discoveries. Celebrating with others who share your passion enhances the joy of collecting and opens doors to new opportunities and friendships.

Now that you've built a collection you can be proud of, think about how you want to preserve and showcase it. Invest in proper storage methods to protect your coins from environmental factors. Perhaps consider creating a display that not only safeguards your treasures but also allows you to share their beauty with others.

Continuing Your Journey in Coin Collecting

As one chapter ends, another begins. Your journey in coin collecting doesn't conclude with this guide—it merely takes a new direction. Consider these steps as you continue to grow and evolve in your numismatic pursuits.

Coin collecting is a vast and ever-evolving field. Stay curious and continue expanding your knowledge. Explore specialized areas, learn about the history behind certain coins, and stay informed about the latest developments in the numismatic world. The more you know, the more enriched your collecting experience becomes.

Don't hesitate to explore new avenues within coin collecting. Whether it's delving into a different era, focusing on a specific type of coin, or diving into the realm of ancient coins, there's always more to discover. Challenge yourself to step outside your comfort zone and embrace the diversity within numismatics.

Consider sharing your passion for coin collecting with others. This could involve introducing friends or family to the hobby, participating in local coin clubs, or even starting your own numismatic blog or social media account. Sharing your experiences can be rewarding and might inspire others to embark on their own coin-collecting journey.

In concluding this guide, remember that coin collecting is not just about the coins; it's about the stories, the history, and the connections you make along the way. Continue to find joy in the pursuit of rare coins, valuable errors, and the fascinating world of numismatics. May your future endeavors in coin collecting be as rewarding as the journey you've embarked upon? Happy collecting!

GLOSSARY

Exploring the world of coin collecting comes with its own set of terms and jargon. Here's a comprehensive glossary to help you navigate the exciting realm of numismatics:

Alloy: A mixture of two or more metals.

American Numismatic Association (ANA): A nonprofit educational organization that encourages the study of money throughout the world.

Annealing: Heating blanks (planchets) in a furnace to soften the metal.

Assay: To analyze and determine the purity of metal.

Bag Mark: A mark on a coin from contact with other coins in a mint bag.

Bi-Metallic: A coin comprised of two different metals, bonded together.

Blank: Another word for planchet, the blank piece of metal on which a coin design is stamped.

Bullion: Platinum, gold, or silver in the form of bars or other storage shapes, including coins and ingots.

Bullion Coin: A precious metal coin traded at current bullion prices.

Business Strike: A coin produced for general circulation, as opposed to a proof or uncirculated coin specially made for collectors.

Bust: A portrait on a coin, usually including the head, neck, and upper shoulders.

Clad Coinage: Coins that have a core and outer layer made of different metals. Since 1965, all circulating U.S. dimes, quarters, half dollars, and dollars have been clad.

Coin: A flat piece of metal issued by the government as money.

Collar: A metal piece that restrains the expanding metal of a planchet during striking.

Commemorative: A special coin or medal issued to honor an outstanding person, place, or event.

Condition: The physical state of a coin.

Counterfeit: A fake coin or other piece of currency made to deceive.

Currency: Any kind of money – coins or paper money – used as a medium of exchange.

Denomination: The different values of money.

Die: An engraved stamp used for impressing a design upon a blank piece of metal to make a coin.

Designer: The artist who creates a coin's design.

Edge: The outer border of a coin, considered the "third side."

Engraver: An artist who sculpts a clay model of a coin's design in bas-relief.

Error: An improperly produced coin released into circulation.

Face Value: The sum for which a coin can be spent or exchanged.

Field: The portion of a coin's surface not used for design or inscription.

Grade: Rating which indicates how much a coin has worn from circulation.

Hairlines: Tiny lines or scratches on coins, usually caused by cleaning or polishing.

Incuse: Opposite of relief, the part of a coin's design that is pressed into the surface.

Ingot: Metal cast into a particular shape; used in making coins.

Inscription: Words stamped on a coin or medal.

Intrinsic Value (Bullion Value): Current market value of the precious metal in a coin.

Key Date: A scarce date required to complete a collection, usually more difficult to find and afford.

Legal Tender: Coins, dollar bills, or other currency issued by a government as official money.

Legend: Principal lettering on a coin.

Medal: A metal object resembling a coin issued to recognize an event, place, person, or group, with no stated value and not intended to circulate as money.

Medium of Exchange: Anything that people agree has a certain value.

Mint: A place where coins of a country are manufactured under government authority.

Mint Luster: The dull, frosty, or satiny shine found on uncirculated coins.

Mint Mark: A small letter on a coin identifying which mint facility struck the coin.

Mint Set: A complete set of coins of each denomination produced by a particular mint.

Mint State: Same as uncirculated.

Mintage: The quantity of coins produced.

Motto: A word, sentence, or phrase inscribed on a coin to express a guiding national principle.

Mylar: Trademark for a polyester film used to store coins.

Numismatics: The study and collecting of things that are used as money.

Obsolete: A coin design or type that is no longer produced.

Obverse: The front (or "heads") side of a coin.

Off-Center: Describes a coin that has received a misaligned strike from the coin press.

Overstrike: A new coin produced with a previously struck coin used as the planchet.

Pattern: An experimental or trial piece, generally of a new design or metal.

Planchet: The blank piece of metal on which a coin design is stamped.

Proof: A specially produced coin made from highly polished planchets and dies.

Proof Set: A complete set of proof coins of each denomination made in a year.

Relief: The part of a coin's design that is raised above the surface.

Restrike: A coin that is minted using the original dies but at a later date.

Reverse: The back (or "tails") side of a coin.

Riddler: A machine that screens out blanks (planchets) that are the wrong size or shape.

Rim: The raised edge on both sides of a coin that helps protect the coin's design from wear.

Roll: Coins packaged by banks, dealers, or the United States Mint.

Series: A collection of coins that contains all date and mint marks of a specific design and denomination.

Slab: Nickname for some protective coin encapsulation methods.

Strike: The process of stamping a coin blank with a design.

Type Set: A collection of coins based on denomination.

Uncirculated: A coin that has not been used in everyday commerce.

Upsetting Mill: A machine that raises the rim on both sides of a blank.

Variety: A minor change from the basic design type of a coin.

Year Set: A collection of all coins issued by a country for any one year.

This glossary serves as your handy companion on your coin collecting journey, helping you decipher the language and delve deeper into the fascinating world of numismatics.

Made in United States
North Haven, CT
11 August 2024